taste of home
THE new
appetizer
the best recipes for today's party starters

REIMAN MEDIA GROUP, INC. • GREENDALE, WISCONSIN

taste of home   Reader's Digest

A TASTE OF HOME/READER'S DIGEST BOOK

Editor in Chief	Catherine Cassidy
Vice President, Executive Editor/Books	Heidi Reuter Lloyd
Creative Director	Ardyth Cope
Food Director	Diane Werner RD
Senior Editor/Books	Mark Hagen
Editor	Janet Briggs
Art Directors	Lori Arndt, Rudy Krochalk
Content Production Supervisor	Julie Wagner
Design Layout Artists	Catherine Fletcher, Kathy Crawford
Proofreader	Linne Bruskewitz
Recipe Asset System	Coleen Martin, Sue A. Jurack
Premedia Supervisor	Scott Berger
Recipe Testing & Editing	Taste of Home Test Kitchen
Food Photography	Taste of Home Photo Studio
Editorial Assistant	Barb Czysz

Chief Marketing Officer:	Lisa Karpinski
Vice President, Book Marketing:	Dan Fink

The Reader's Digest Association, Inc.

President and Chief Executive Officer	Mary G. Berner
President, RDA Food & Entertaining	Suzanne M. Grimes
President, Consumer Marketing	Dawn Zier

Pictured on front cover (clockwise from bottom right): Party Pesto Pinwheels (p. 73),
Crab-Stuffed Cherry Tomatoes (p. 173), Artichoke Crostini (p. 186),
Veggie Wonton Quiches (p. 57) and Beer Cheese (p. 24).

Pictured on back cover (from top to bottom): Spicy Summer Sub (p. 84),
Veggie Shrimp Egg Rolls (p. 66) and Cheese-Filled Shortbread Tart (p. 240).

International Standard Book Number (10): 0-89821-728-8
International Standard Book Number (13): 978-0-89821-728-5
Library of Congress Control Number: 2008943192

"Timeless Recipes from Trusted Home Cooks" is a registered trademark of Reiman Media Group, Inc.

For other Taste of Home books and products, visit www.tasteofhome.com.
For more Reader's Digest products and information, visit
www.rd.com (in the United States)
www.rd.ca (in Canada).

Printed in China.
5 7 9 10 8 6 4

table of contents

THE **new** appetizer

With 230 satisfying dips, spreads, wraps, rolls, pizzas, nibblers, munchies, sweets and more in this fabulous collection of bite-size goodies, you'll be the hostess that serves the most sensational assortment of appetizers!

EVERYONE LOVES THE OPPORTUNITY TO SAMPLE DIFFERENT AND DELICIOUS foods at parties and gatherings. And appetizers are the tastiest way to tempt your guests and introduce them to fun, new flavors. Now you can serve up 230 of the most delectable dips and spreads, juicy chicken wings, dainty canapes, mouth-watering finger foods, and scrumptious desserts—all easy to make and a delight to serve!

All the recipes in this collection come from good cooks like you and have been tested by the experienced home economists in the Taste of Home Test Kitchen. So you can rest assured that these bite-size goodies will be a savory success.

In this big book, you'll also discover make-ahead preparation tips, practical pointers for keeping party foods hot or cold, helpful hints for serving appetizers, time-saving tips and much more.

So turn to *The New Appetizer* for an abundance of appealing appetizers…and make your next party a celebration of flavor!

Serving Up Appetizers

When you offer friends and family appetizers or snacks, you invite them to get comfortable and share time with you and other guests.

Appetizers can be as simple as dip with chips for a casual night of TV watching, include heartier fare, like sandwiches and pizza for Sunday football, serve as a first course to a festive meal, entertain a large group at an open house or even be the main meal for a special occasion.

Party Planning

Whether simple or fancy, savory or sweet, hot or cold, appetizers offer versatility and variety when entertaining. And as an added benefit, many appetizers can be made ahead of time—some even weeks in advance and then frozen—so you can be ready for guests at a moment's notice or relaxed when party time arrives.

When planning what appetizers to serve, don't overdo it. It's better to prepare a few good choices than to stress over making a lot of items. Start with one spectacular appetizer and then build your menu with other easy but delicious foods.

Choose from hot, cold and room temperature foods. Select recipes that offer a variety of colors, textures (soft and crunchy) and flavors (sour, salty, savory, sweet, spicy or subtle). Mix in one or two lighter options to cater to guests concerned about calories or fat. And, look for appetizers that make a nice presentation and require no last-minute fussing.

How Much To Serve

The number of appetizers per person varies on the length of the party, the number of guests and the purpose of the appetizers.

For a social hour before dinner, plan on serving three or four different appetizers and allow four to five pieces per person.

For an open-house affair, plan on serving four to five different appetizers and allow four to six pieces per person per hour.

For an appetizer buffet that is served in place of a meal, plan on serving six to eight different appetizers and allow 10 to 14 pieces per person.

In general, for larger groups you should offer more types of appetizers. For eight guests, three types may be sufficient, 16 guests about four to five types and for 25 guests, serve six to eight types. The more variety of appetizers you serve, the fewer servings of each type each person will take.

Food Quantities for Appetizers

When serving appetizers, no one wants to run out of food. But the dilemma is to know how much will be enough. Here are some guidelines to estimate how much you'll need per person. The larger the variety of appetizers you serve, the less of each type you will need.

appetizers	beverages (per hour)	miscellaneous
3 tablespoons dips	In warm weather, you may wish to have additional chilled beverages.	1 to 2 ounces chips
2 ounces cheese		4 crackers
3 to 4 cocktail wieners		4 fruit or vegetable dippers
1 to 2 ounces deli meat	1 to 2 cups soda, water or iced tea	1/2 ounce mixed nuts
3 tablespoons dips	6 ounces juice	3 to 4 pickle slices or 1 pickle spear
2 to 4 small egg rolls	1 to 2 bottles beer	
3 to 4 meatballs	1/2 (750-ml) bottle wine	3 to 4 olives
1 to 2 slices pizza	3/4 cup hot coffee or tea	1 to 2 small rolls
2 to 4 miniature quiches	1/2 cup punch	3 to 4 ounces ice for beverages

Points About Food Safety

The general guideline when serving food is that cooked foods and uncooked foods that require refrigeration should not sit out at room temperature for more than 2 hours or 1 hour on hot days (90° or above). Hot foods should be kept hot (140°) and cold foods should be kept cold (40°). Here are some pointers for safely serving food:

- Divide the food among several serving dishes. Serve one dish, while the others are being chilled or kept warm. Replace the original serving dish as needed or every two hours whichever comes first.

- To keep foods hot when serving, use insulated containers, warming trays, slow cookers or chafing dishes.

- To keep the back up food hot, arrange on baking sheets and place in a 200° oven.

- To keep food cold, place on ice. You can easily improvise an ice bowl by placing dips, shrimp, cut-up fruits and salads in a bowl. Then set the bowl in a larger one filled with ice cubes or crushed ice. Replenish ice for chilling as it melts.

Hosting an Appetizer Party

Although hosting an appetizer party will require some planning, it's a fun way to entertain a group of people for any occasion.

To make it easy on you, include several make-ahead recipes on the menu.

A few weeks before the party:
Cook and freeze meatballs, savory cheesecakes and puffs or mini quiches, such as Crabmeat Appetizer Cheesecake (p. 30) or Mini Bacon Quiches (p. 77). For meatballs, just thaw and reheat in the sauce on your party day. For savory cheesecakes, thaw in the refrigerator 2 to 3 days before the party and bring to room temperature about 20 minutes before serving. Puffs and quiches can be reheated in a 300° oven until warm just before guests arrive.

A few days before the party:
Make cheese balls and logs, flavored nut mixes and snack mixes. Store the mixes in airtight containers.

A day before the party:
Make tortilla-type roll-up sandwiches, dips and salsas. Cut up any fruit and vegetables that will be used for dippers. Prep any fillings for hot appetizers or any other food that can be made ahead.

The morning of your party:
Make hero-type sandwiches and assemble canapes. If possible, assemble and arrange any warm appetizers on baking sheets.

Before your guests arrive:
Place any long-cooking items, such as a baked dip in a bread shell, in the oven so that it will be ready to serve within half an hour after the party starts.

As the guests arrive:
Place some of the quickly baked items in the oven.

Arranging The Food

They way you arrange your food will encourage people to mingle with each other and move around your home. Food can be set up as a buffet, served from trays by waitstaff or family, or casually placed throughout the house on tables. To keep people moving, set up the food and beverages in separate locations—even in separate rooms.

Buffets

For added visual interest to a buffet service, arrange various items such as a phone book, sturdy boxes, inverted metal buckets, cake pans and cans, as risers on your table (see figure 1). Drape them with a tablecloth and gently form it around the risers so that the cloth won't pull when platters of food are set on top (see figure 2).

When arranging the buffet, allow room on one end for the plates, and set the napkins and any utensils on the other end. This way your guests won't need to juggle the napkin and utensils while they serve themselves. Set the food back from the edge of the table to allow room for guests to set their plates down to serve themselves. For foods that need to be skewered, have a container of skewers or toothpicks alongside the serving dish.

If using candles, set them on the table so no one will need to reach over the flames to get the food. Small arrangements of flowers can be placed between serving dishes (see figure 3). Large arrangements should be placed out of reach, either in the middle of the buffet if service wraps around the table, or in the back if your table is against a wall.

If you're using a table for the buffet, remove the chairs from the table and arrange them in other areas in sitting groups. By removing the chairs, you discourage guests from sitting at the buffet and encourage them to mingle.

Trays

Trays can be used to circulate the food among the guests. This can be especially nice for hot finger foods, such as stuffed mushrooms or canapes. Offering food directly to people encourages them to sample the food. The trays will be emptied in a short period of time, eliminating concerns about food standing at room

Figure 1

Figure 2

Figure 3

temperature too long. Plus, the trays can easily be replenished with fresh tidbits.

For the best visual presentation, only place one or two types of food on a tray. Leave space around the food to prevent other pieces on the tray from being touched when one piece is picked up. Small tongs can aid in serving the appetizers from the tray. Or, if appropriate, use individual party picks with foods such as cubed cheese. Since the trays are being carried around, avoid making them too heavy. If you don't have enough trays for the occasion, consider renting them.

Placing Food Around the House

Placing appetizers in various locations throughout the party area invites people to walk around to see what other tasty bites are being served and, most importantly, to meet other guests. Scattered placement around the party area can work well with room temperature foods, chilled items and platters of hot appetizers. For items that need a slow cooker or chafing dish, a central location may be more convenient.

Tips to Make Guests Comfortable

Simple touches can enhance the comfort of your guests. Here's a few tips to make your party even more enjoyable:

- Have music in the background to set the mood and still allow conversations to take place at a normal tone.
- Have chairs for people to sit (not everyone can stand for hours).
- Place the chairs in seating arrangements to encourage conversation.
- If you want your guests to use coasters, have plenty of them available, and place them in noticeable locations.
- Have small tables and open surfaces on other furniture, where a guest may set down their glass or plate.
- Have an open floor plan so guests can easily walk from one room to the next.
- Have trash containers strategically placed around the area to prevent clutter from building up.

spread it on

Warm from the oven or straight from the refrigerator, spreads and dips are guaranteed crowd-pleasers. Just choose from Baked Onion Brie Spread (p. 18), Mixed Fruit Salsa (p. 17) or Roasted Goat Cheese with Garlic (p. 43).

Because many take just minutes to whip up, they are tasty party must-haves. When time's tight serve alongside store-bought dippers, such as crackers, bagel chips, potato chips or tortilla chips. For more nutritious options, cut up an assortment of fresh fruits and vegetables.

brie with apricot topping

½ cup chopped dried apricots

2 tablespoons brown sugar

2 tablespoons water

1 teaspoon balsamic vinegar

Dash salt

½ to 1 teaspoon minced fresh rosemary *or* ¼ teaspoon dried rosemary, crushed

1 round Brie cheese (8 ounces)

Assorted crackers

1 In a small saucepan, combine the apricots, brown sugar, water, vinegar and salt. Bring to a boil. Reduce heat to medium; cook and stir until slightly thickened. Remove from the heat; stir in rosemary.

2 Remove rind from top of cheese. Place in an ungreased ovenproof serving dish. Spread apricot mixture over cheese. Bake, uncovered, at 400° for 10-12 minutes or until cheese is softened. Serve with crackers.

YIELD: 6-8 SERVINGS.

Taste of Home Test Kitchen

Folks will think you fussed over this pretty appetizer, but it takes only minutes to top a round of smooth and creamy brie with warm sweet apricots. This is one easy appetizer certain to make any occasion special.

sun-dried tomato-flavored hummus

1 can (15 ounces) garbanzo beans *or* chickpeas, rinsed and drained

1/3 cup reduced-fat mayonnaise

1 tablespoon sun-dried tomato pesto sauce mix

1 teaspoon lemon juice

Assorted crackers

In a food processor or blender, combine the beans, mayonnaise, sauce mix and lemon juice; cover and process until blended. Transfer to a small bowl. Serve with crackers. Store in the refrigerator.

YIELD: 1 1/4 CUPS.

EDITOR'S NOTE: This recipe was tested with Knorr Sun-Dried Tomato Pesto Sauce.

Kathleen Tribble, Buellton, California

I didn't like the hummus I bought in a box mix or in refrigerated tubs, so I made my own version using a pesto sauce mix. My husband and I enjoy it in sandwiches, but it's great on crackers, too. We like it so much that we eat any leftovers with a spoon!

walnut chicken spread

1 3/4 cups finely chopped cooked chicken

1 cup finely chopped walnuts

2/3 cup mayonnaise

1 celery rib, finely chopped

1 small onion, finely chopped

1 teaspoon salt

1/2 teaspoon garlic powder

Assorted crackers

In a bowl, combine the chicken, walnuts, mayonnaise, celery, onion, salt and garlic powder. Serve with crackers.

YIELD: 2 1/2 CUPS.

Joan Whelan, Green Valley, Arizona

It's a breeze to stir together this tasty chicken spread. We enjoy the mild combination of chicken, crunchy walnuts, onion and celery. It's perfect with crackers or as a sandwich filling.

calico corn salsa

Jennifer Gardner, Sandy, Utah

A friend gave me the recipe for this colorful salsa, and when I took it to a luncheon, everyone loved it. This recipe makes 4 cups, but is easily doubled for larger gatherings.

1½ cups frozen corn, thawed

1 cup frozen peas, thawed

½ teaspoon ground cumin

⅛ teaspoon dried oregano

1 tablespoon olive oil

1 can (15 ounces) black beans, rinsed and drained

1 medium tomato, chopped

⅓ cup chopped red onion

¼ cup lime juice

1 tablespoon Dijon mustard

1 garlic clove, minced

½ teaspoon salt

2 tablespoons minced fresh cilantro

Tortilla chips

1 In a large bowl, combine the corn and peas. In a nonstick skillet, cook cumin and oregano in oil over medium heat for 2 minutes. Pour over corn mixture; stir to coat evenly. Stir in the beans, tomato and onion.

2 In a small bowl, whisk the lime juice, mustard, garlic and salt. Stir in cilantro. Pour over corn mixture and stir to coat. Serve with tortilla chips. Refrigerate leftovers.

YIELD: 4 CUPS.

festive vegetable dip

1 cup mayonnaise

½ cup sour cream

2 tablespoons minced fresh parsley

1 tablespoon minced chives

1 teaspoon dried minced onion

½ teaspoon lemon juice

½ teaspoon Worcestershire sauce

¼ teaspoon salt

¼ teaspoon paprika

⅛ teaspoon curry powder

⅛ teaspoon pepper

1 medium green pepper

1 medium sweet red pepper

Assorted raw vegetables

1 In a large bowl, combine the first 11 ingredients. Cover and refrigerate for at least 1 hour.

2 Lay green pepper on its side; with a sharp knife, make a horizontal slice just above stem. Remove top piece; save for another use. Remove membrane and seeds. Repeat with red pepper. Fill peppers with dip. Serve with vegetables.

YIELD: 1½ CUPS.

Mary Pollard, Crossville, Tennessee

I like to serve this well-seasoned dip with veggies. It rounds out a holiday snack buffet in a festive way when it's served in hollowed-out green and red bell peppers.

mixed fruit salsa

1 package (16 ounces) mixed frozen berries, thawed and chopped

2 medium peaches, diced

2 medium kiwifruit, peeled and diced

3 tablespoons sugar

2 tablespoons lemon juice

1½ teaspoons grated lime peel

CINNAMON TORTILLA CHIPS:

8 flour tortillas (7 inches)

3 tablespoons butter, melted

3 tablespoons sugar

1½ teaspoons ground cinnamon

1 In a large bowl, combine the first six ingredients; set aside. Brush both sides of tortillas with butter. Combine the sugar and cinnamon; sprinkle over both sides of tortilla. Cut each into six wedges.

2 Place on ungreased baking sheets. Bake at 400° for 6-8 minutes on each side or until crisp. Drain salsa; serve with tortilla chips.

YIELD: 6-8 SERVINGS.

Laura Loncour, Milwaukee, Wisconsin

For a unique salsa, this recipes tosses frozen berries with fresh peaches and kiwifruit. You can use canned peaches instead of fresh. It's a terrific snack or dessert served with homemade cinnamon tortilla chips.

baked onion brie spread

1 large onion, chopped

2 tablespoons minced garlic

2 tablespoons butter

1 round (8 ounces) Brie *or* Camembert cheese, rind removed and cubed

1 package (8 ounces) cream cheese, cubed

¾ cup sour cream

2 teaspoons brown sugar

2 teaspoons lemon juice

1 teaspoon Worcestershire sauce

⅛ teaspoon salt

⅛ teaspoon pepper

1 round loaf (1 pound) sourdough bread

Paprika

Fresh vegetables

1 In a large skillet, cook onion and garlic in butter over medium heat for 8-10 minutes or until onion is golden brown, stirring frequently. Remove from the heat; set aside.

2 Place Brie and cream cheese in a microwave-safe dish. Microwave, uncovered, until softened. Whisk in the sour cream, brown sugar, lemon juice, Worcestershire sauce, salt, pepper and onion mixture.

3 Cut top off loaf of bread; set aside. Hollow out loaf, leaving a ¾-in. shell. Cut removed bread into cubes. Fill shell with cheese mixture; replace top. Wrap in a large piece of heavy-duty foil (about 18 in. square). Place on a baking sheet.

4 Bake at 400° for 1 hour or until spread is bubbly. Remove top of bread. Sprinkle paprika over spread. Serve with bread cubes and vegetables.

YIELD: 2¾ CUPS.

Lori Adams, Mooresville, Indiana

The buttery brie-and-onion flavor of this spread just melts in your mouth. Plus, you can even eat the bread bowl, which my husband says is the best part!

caramel peanut butter dip

30 caramels

1 to 2 tablespoons water

¼ cup plus 2 tablespoons creamy peanut butter

¼ cup finely crushed peanuts, optional

Sliced apples

In a microwave-safe bowl, microwave the caramels and water on high for 1 minute; stir. Microwave 1 minute longer or until smooth. Add peanut butter and mix well; microwave for 30 seconds or until smooth. Stir peanuts if desired. Serve warm with apples.

YIELD: 1 CUP.

Sandra McKenzie, Braham, Minnesota

When crisp autumn apples are available, I quickly use them up when I serve this quick delicious dip.

chutney cheddar spread

4 ounces cheddar cheese, cubed

¼ cup chutney

2 tablespoons butter, softened

1 tablespoon finely chopped onion

¼ teaspoon Worcestershire sauce

Dash hot pepper sauce

Assorted crackers

In a food processor, combine the first six ingredients; cover and process until mixture achieves spreading consistency. Refrigerate until serving. Serve with crackers.

YIELD: ABOUT 1 CUP.

Regina Costlow, East Brady, Pennsylvania

This appetizer can be whipped together in minutes with ingredients I have on hand in the kitchen.

cider cheese fondue

¾ cup apple cider *or* apple juice

2 cups (8 ounces) shredded cheddar cheese

1 cup (4 ounces) shredded Swiss cheese

1 tablespoon cornstarch

⅛ teaspoon pepper

1 loaf (1 pound) French bread, cut into cubes

In a large saucepan, bring cider to a boil. Reduce heat to medium-low. Toss the cheeses with cornstarch and pepper; stir into cider. Cook and stir for 3-4 minutes or until cheese is melted. Transfer to a small ceramic fondue pot or slow cooker; keep warm. Serve with bread cubes.

YIELD: 2⅔ CUPS.

Kim Marie Van Rheenen, Mendota, Illinois

Cheese lovers are sure to enjoy dipping into this creamy, quick-to-fix fondue that has just a hint of apple. You can also serve this appetizer with apple or pear wedges.

sweet cheese ball

2 packages (8 ounces *each*) cream cheese, softened

½ cup confectioners' sugar

⅔ cup flaked coconut

8 maraschino cherries, finely chopped

¾ cup finely chopped pecans

Assorted fresh fruit

In a small mixing bowl, beat cream cheese and confectioners' sugar until smooth. Beat in the coconut and cherries. Shape into a ball; roll in pecans. Cover and refrigerate until serving. Serve with fruit.

YIELD: 1 CHEESE BALL (3½ CUPS).

Melissa Friend, Oakland, Maryland
You'll need only a few items for this unique cheese ball. Coconut comes through in the cherry-flecked mixture that's coated in pecans. It looks pretty and tastes delicious served with apple slices, pineapple wedges, berries and other fresh fruit.

baked spinach dip in bread

Shauna Dittrick, Leduc, Alberta

This is the only way my kids will eat spinach! The dip can be made ahead and chilled. Place in the bread shell and bake just before company arrives.

2 packages (8 ounces *each*) cream cheese, softened

1 cup mayonnaise

1 package (10 ounces) frozen chopped spinach, thawed and squeezed dry

1 cup (4 ounces) shredded cheddar cheese

1 pound sliced bacon, cooked and crumbled

1/4 cup chopped onion

1 tablespoon dill weed

1 to 2 garlic cloves, minced

1 round loaf (1 pound) unsliced sourdough bread

Assorted fresh vegetables

1 In a large mixing bowl, beat the cream cheese and mayonnaise until blended. Stir in the spinach, cheese, bacon, onion, dill and garlic; set aside.

2 Cut a 1½-in. slice off top of bread; set aside. Carefully hollow out bottom, leaving a ½-in. shell. Cube removed bread and place on a baking sheet. Broil 3-4 in. from the heat for 1-2 minutes or until golden brown; set aside.

3 Fill bread shell with spinach dip; replace top. Place any dip that doesn't fit in shell in a greased baking dish. Wrap in a large piece of heavy-duty foil (about 18 in. square). Place on a baking sheet.

4 Bake at 350° for 1 hour or until dip is heated through. Cover and bake additional dip for 40-45 minutes or until heated through. Open foil carefully. Serve dip warm with vegetables and reserved bread cubes.

YIELD: 4 CUPS.

EDITOR'S NOTE: Fat-free cream cheese and mayonnaise are not recommended for this recipe.

beer cheese

⅓ cup beer *or* nonalcoholic beer

4 ounces cream cheese, cubed

3 ounces crumbled blue cheese

¼ cup Dijon mustard

2 tablespoons grated onion

½ to 1 teaspoon hot pepper sauce

1 garlic clove, minced

3 cups (12 ounces) shredded cheddar cheese

Assorted crackers

1 In a small saucepan, bring beer to a boil. Remove from the heat and cool to room temperature.

2 In a food processor, combine the beer, cream cheese, blue cheese, mustard, onion, hot pepper sauce and garlic. Add cheddar cheese; cover and process until well blended. Transfer to a bowl. Cover and refrigerate overnight.

3 Let cheese stand at room temperature for 30 minutes before serving. Serve with crackers.

YIELD: 3 CUPS.

Pat Wartman, Bethlehem, Pennsylvania

I like to serve this zesty cheese spread with crackers and veggie dippers. It's great to take along to picnics.

roasted eggplant dip

1 medium eggplant (about 1 pound)

9 green onions (white portion only)

3 tablespoons reduced-fat plain yogurt

1 tablespoon lemon juice

1 tablespoon olive oil

1/2 teaspoon salt

1/4 teaspoon pepper

3 tablespoons minced chives, *divided*

Pita breads (6 inches), cut into 6 wedges

Carrot sticks, optional

1 Pierce eggplant several times with a fork. Place eggplant and onions in a shallow foil-lined baking pan. Bake at 400° for 25-30 minutes or until tender. Cool. Peel and cube the eggplant.

2 In a blender or food processor, combine the yogurt, lemon juice, oil, salt, pepper, eggplant and onions. Cover and process until almost smooth. Add 2 tablespoons chives; cover and process until blended.

3 Transfer to a serving bowl; sprinkle with remaining chives. Serve with pita wedges and carrots if desired.

YIELD: 1½ CUPS.

Nina Hall, Spokane, Washington

Here's a fun way to use some of your garden-fresh eggplant crop. This chunky guacamole-like dip—seasoned with lemon juice, onions and chives—goes great with pita wedges or melba toast.

ham cream cheese balls

2 packages (8 ounces *each*) cream cheese, softened

1 package (2½ ounces) thinly sliced deli ham, finely chopped

3 green onions, finely chopped

2 tablespoons Worcestershire sauce

1 cup finely chopped peanuts

Crackers and raw vegetables

In a bowl, combine the cream cheese, ham, onions and Worcestershire sauce; mix well. Shape into ¾-in. balls. Roll in peanuts. Cover and refrigerate until serving. Serve with crackers and vegetables.

YIELD: ABOUT 5 DOZEN.

Jill Kirby, Calhoun, Georgia

It seems like I'm always hosting a shower, birthday or other celebration. This spread is fast to fix.

hot and spicy cranberry dip

1 can (16 ounces) jellied cranberry sauce

2 to 3 tablespoons prepared horseradish

2 tablespoons honey

1 tablespoon Worcestershire sauce

1 tablespoon lemon juice

1 garlic clove, minced

1/4 to 1/2 teaspoon ground cayenne pepper

Dippers: pineapple chunks, orange sections and warmed mini fully cooked sausages

In a medium saucepan, combine first seven ingredients. Bring to a boil. Reduce heat; cover and simmer for 5 minutes. Serve warm with the pineapple, oranges and sausages.

YIELD: 2 CUPS.

Dorothy Pritchett, Wills Point, Texas

This savory dipping sauce has a festive red color and is packed with lots of flavor.

---

chorizo cheese dip

½ pound uncooked chorizo, casings removed

1 small green pepper, chopped

1 small sweet red pepper, chopped

1 small onion, chopped

3 garlic cloves, minced

1 tablespoon vegetable oil

½ teaspoon cayenne pepper

2 cartons (12 ounces *each*) white Mexican dipping cheese

Tortilla chips

1 In a large skillet, cook chorizo over medium heat until no longer pink; drain. Remove and keep warm. In the same skillet, saute the peppers, onion and garlic in oil until tender. Stir in cayenne and chorizo; heat through.

2 Heat cheese according to package directions; stir into meat mixture. Serve warm with tortilla chips. Refrigerate leftovers.

YIELD: 4 CUPS.

Taste of Home Test Kitchen

Guests will wipe the bowl clean when you set out this spicy cheese dip. Serve it with tortilla chips and vegetable dippers.

texas caviar

1 can (15½ ounces) black-eyed peas, rinsed and drained

¾ cup chopped sweet red pepper

¾ cup chopped green pepper

1 medium onion, chopped

3 green onions, chopped

¼ cup minced fresh parsley

1 jar (2 ounces) diced pimientos, drained

1 garlic clove, minced

1 bottle (8 ounces) fat-free Italian salad dressing

Tortilla chips

In a large bowl, combine the peas, peppers, onions, parsley, pimientos and garlic. Pour salad dressing over pea mixture; stir gently to coat. Cover and refrigerate for 24 hours. Serve with tortilla chips.

YIELD: 4 CUPS.

Kathy Faris, Lytle, Texas

My neighbor gave me a container of this zippy, tangy salsa one Christmas and I had to have the recipe. I fix it regularly for potlucks and get-togethers and never have any left over. I bring copies of the recipe with me whenever I take the salsa.

hot seafood spread

1 package (8 ounces) cream cheese, softened

2 cups (8 ounces) shredded cheddar cheese

1 cup mayonnaise

1 can (4¼ ounces) tiny shrimp, rinsed and drained

¾ cup imitation crabmeat, chopped

½ cup chopped green onions

¼ cup grated Parmesan cheese

2 teaspoons dill weed

2 teaspoons minced fresh parsley

1 round loaf (1½ pounds) unsliced bread

Assorted fresh vegetables

1 In a mixing bowl, combine the first nine ingredients. Cut the top fourth off the loaf of bread; carefully hollow out bottom, leaving a ½-in. shell. Cube removed bread; set aside. Fill bread shell with seafood mixture.

2 Place on an ungreased baking sheet. Cover top edges loosely with foil. Bake at 350° for 25 minutes. Remove foil; bake 25-35 minutes longer or until crust is golden brown and spread is heated through. Serve with vegetables and bread cubes.

YIELD: 4 CUPS.

EDITOR'S NOTE: Fat-free cream cheese and mayonnaise are not recommended for this recipe.

Linda Doll, St. Albert, Alberta

This creamy, flavorful dip is sure to be popular at parties. Bake it in a hollowed-out pumpernickel or white round bread loaf. Serve it with bread cubes, pita bread or assorted raw veggies. Sometimes I use canned crab instead of the imitation crabmeat.

crabmeat appetizer cheesecake

Andrea MacIntire, Delaware Water Gap, Pennsylvania

I found a lobster cheesecake recipe and decided to come up with my own version using crabmeat instead. It tastes great, so now I make it often!

½ cup seasoned bread crumbs

½ cup grated Parmesan cheese

¼ cup butter, melted

FILLING:

¼ cup *each* chopped sweet red, yellow and green pepper

¼ cup chopped onion

¼ cup butter

4 packages (three 8 ounces, one 3 ounces) cream cheese, softened

3 eggs, lightly beaten

2 cups heavy whipping cream

2 cups canned crabmeat, drained, flaked and cartilage removed

2 cups (8 ounces) shredded Swiss cheese

½ teaspoon salt

1 In a bowl, combine bread crumbs, Parmesan cheese and butter. Press onto the bottom of a 10-in. springform pan; set aside. In a skillet, saute peppers and onion in butter until tender; set aside.

2 In a mixing bowl, beat cream cheese until smooth. Add eggs; beat on low speed just until combined. Stir in the cream, crab, Swiss cheese, pepper mixture and salt. Pour over crust.

3 Place pan on a baking sheet. Bake at 325° for 60-65 minutes or until center is almost set. Cool on a wire rack for 10 minutes. Carefully run a knife around edge of pan to loosen. Cool for 1 hour longer. Refrigerate overnight.

4 Remove sides of pan. Let stand at room temperature for 30 minutes before serving. Refrigerate leftovers.

YIELD: 16-18 SERVINGS.

ten-minute zesty salsa

1 can (10 ounces) diced tomatoes and green chilies, undrained

1 tablespoon seeded chopped jalapeno pepper

1 tablespoon chopped red onion

1 tablespoon minced fresh cilantro

1 garlic clove, minced

1 tablespoon olive oil

Dash salt

Dash pepper

Tortilla chips

In a small bowl, combine the tomatoes, jalapeno, onion, cilantro, garlic, oil, salt and pepper. Refrigerate until serving. Serve with tortilla chips.

YIELD: 1½ CUPS.

EDITOR'S NOTE: When cutting or seeding hot peppers, use rubber or plastic gloves to protect your hands. Avoid touching your face.

Kim Morin, Lake George, Colorado

The view from our mountain home includes Pikes Peak, so we frequently eat on our wraparound porch when the weather is good. During family get-togethers, we often savor this zippy salsa with chips while we feast on the natural beauty all around us.

lobster spread

1 package (8 ounces) cream cheese, softened

1 tablespoon milk

1½ cups flaked lobster *or* crabmeat

2 tablespoons chopped onion

½ teaspoon horseradish

¼ teaspoon salt

Dash pepper

Paprika

¼ cup sliced almonds

Assorted crackers

In a bowl, combine cream cheese and milk until smooth. Add the lobster, onion, horseradish, salt and pepper. Spread into a greased 8-in. ovenproof dish. Sprinkle with paprika and almonds. Bake at 375° for about 15 minutes until bubbly. Serve warm with assorted crackers.

YIELD: 2¾ CUPS.

Jeff and Judi Burke, Isle au Haut, Maine
We like to enjoy this with crispy whole wheat crackers. It's always a hit when we serve it, and it takes only a few minute to whip up.

feta olive dip

4 ounces reduced-fat cream cheese

½ cup crumbled feta cheese

½ cup reduced-fat sour cream

¼ cup sliced ripe olives

2 garlic cloves, minced

2 teaspoons dried oregano

1 teaspoon minced fresh parsley

¼ teaspoon salt

¼ to ½ teaspoon hot pepper sauce

Baked pita chips

In a food processor or blender, combine the first nine ingredients; cover and process until blended. Transfer to a bowl. Cover and refrigerate for at least 1 hour before serving. Serve with pita chips.

YIELD: ABOUT 1½ CUPS.

Debbie Burton, Callander, Ontario
Feta cheese, garlic and ripe olives, along with a hint of hot sauce, give a Greek salad-like flavor to this distinctive dip. Besides pita chips, it's terrific with crackers, tortilla chips, pita bread, pretzels and carrot and celery sticks.

six-layer dip

2 medium ripe avocados, peeled and sliced

2 tablespoons lemon juice

1/2 tablespoon garlic salt

1/8 teaspoon hot pepper sauce

1 cup (8 ounces) sour cream

1 can (2 1/4 ounces) chopped ripe olives, drained

1 jar (16 ounces) thick and chunky salsa, drained

2 medium tomatoes, seeded and chopped

1 cup (8 ounces) shredded cheddar cheese

Tortilla chips

In a large bowl, mash the avocados with lemon juice, garlic salt and hot pepper sauce. Spoon into a deep-dish 10-in. pie plate or serving bowl. Layer with the sour cream, olives, salsa, tomatoes and cheese. Cover and refrigerate for at least 1 hour. Serve with chips.

YIELD: 2 1/2 CUPS.

Etta Gillespie, San Angelo, Texas

Tortilla chips make great scoopers for this dip, which is a family favorite after we open Christmas gifts. Sometimes I serve it in a glass bowl—just to show off the pretty layers.

raspberry cheese spread

4 ounces cream cheese, softened

1 cup mayonnaise

2 cups (8 ounces) shredded part-skim mozzarella cheese

2 cups (8 ounces) shredded cheddar cheese

3 green onions, finely chopped

1 cup chopped pecans

¼ cup seedless raspberry preserves

Assorted crackers

1 In a small mixing bowl, beat the cream cheese and mayonnaise until blended. Beat in cheeses and onions. Stir in pecans. Spread into a plastic wrap-lined 9-in. round dish. Refrigerate until set, about 1 hour.

2 Invert onto a serving plate; spread with preserves. Serve with crackers.

YIELD: ABOUT 3½ CUPS.

Jane Montgomery, Hilliard, Ohio

A party guest brought this attractive appetizer to our home, and we fell in love with it. Now I often make it myself when we have company.

tiered cheese slices

1 package (8 ounces) cream cheese, softened

½ teaspoon hot pepper sauce

¼ teaspoon salt

¼ cup chopped pecans

¼ cup dried cranberries

2 packages (8 ounces *each*) deli-style cheddar cheese slices (about 3 inches square)

Assorted crackers

1 In a mixing bowl, combine the cream cheese, hot pepper sauce and salt. Stir in pecans and cranberries.

2 On a 12-in. square of aluminum foil, place two slices of cheese side by side; spread with 2-3 tablespoons cream cheese mixture. Repeat layers six times. Top with two cheese slices. (Save remaining cheese slices for another use.)

3 Fold foil around cheese and seal tightly. Refrigerate for 8 hours or overnight. Cut in half lengthwise and then widthwise into ¼-in. slices. Serve with crackers.

YIELD: ABOUT 4 DOZEN.

Diane Benjaminson, Coleville, Saskatchewan

I can't tell you how many times I've made this recipe or been asked to share it! Guests always think I fussed, but the simple ingredients go together in minutes using presliced cheese. For busy holiday hostesses, it's a do-ahead delight.

dijon chicken liver pate

½ pound bulk pork sausage

1 small onion, chopped

½ pound chicken livers, cut in half

⅓ cup milk

2 tablespoons Dijon mustard

1 package (8 ounces) cream cheese, softened

½ teaspoon garlic powder

¼ teaspoon *each* minced chives, dried parsley flakes, tarragon and marjoram

Assorted crackers

1 In a large skillet, cook sausage and onion over medium heat until meat is no longer pink; remove with a slotted spoon and set aside. In the drippings, cook chicken livers over medium heat for 6-8 minutes or until no longer pink. Drain; cool for 10 minutes.

2 Place chicken livers, milk and mustard in a blender or food processor; cover and process. Add the sausage mixture, cream cheese and seasonings; cover and process until nearly smooth.

3 Pour into a 3-cup serving bowl. Cover and refrigerate for 6 hours or overnight. Serve with crackers.

YIELD: 3 CUPS.

Katherine Wells, Brodhead, Wisconsin

I first served this chicken liver pate at a holiday party quite a few years ago, and it was a real hit. The special flavoring comes from cream cheese, mustard and pork sausage.

salsa guacamole

6 small ripe avocados, halved, pitted and peeled

¼ cup lemon juice

1 cup salsa

2 green onions, finely chopped

¼ teaspoon salt *or* salt-free seasoning blend

¼ teaspoon garlic powder

Tortilla chips

In a bowl, mash avocados with lemon juice. Stir in the salsa, onions, salt and garlic powder. Serve immediately with tortilla chips.

YIELD: 4 CUPS.

Lauren Heyn, Oak Creek, Wisconsin

I've never tasted better guacamole than this. If there's time, I make homemade tortilla chips by frying 1-inch strips of flour tortillas in oil and salting them.

warm asparagus-crab spread

Camille Wisniewski, Jackson, New Jersey

When my children entertain, I like to help them with the cooking. This warm and flavorful dip is a favorite contribution of mine. Cashew nuts give this creamy mixture a nice crunch.

1 medium sweet red pepper, chopped

3 green onions, sliced

2 medium jalapeno peppers, seeded and finely chopped

2 teaspoons vegetable oil

1 can (15 ounces) asparagus spears, drained and chopped

2 cans (6 ounces *each*) crabmeat, drained, flaked and cartilage removed

1 cup mayonnaise

1/2 cup grated *or* shredded Parmesan cheese

1/2 cup chopped cashews

Assorted crackers

1 In a large skillet, saute the red pepper, onions and jalapenos in oil until tender. Add the asparagus, crab, mayonnaise and Parmesan cheese; mix well.

2 Transfer to a greased 1-qt. baking dish. Sprinkle with cashews. Bake, uncovered, at 375° for 20-25 minutes or until bubbly. Serve with crackers.

YIELD: 3 CUPS.

EDITOR'S NOTE: Reduced-fat or fat-free mayonnaise is not recommended for this recipe. When cutting or seeding hot peppers, use rubber or plastic gloves to protect your hands. Avoid touching your face.

hot artichoke spread

1 can (14 ounces) water-packed artichoke hearts, rinsed, drained and chopped

1 cup mayonnaise

1 cup grated Parmesan cheese

1 can (4 ounces) chopped green chilies, drained

1 garlic clove, minced

1 cup chopped fresh tomatoes

3 green onions, thinly sliced

Crackers *or* pita bread

1 In a large bowl, combine the first five ingredients. Spread into a 1-qt. baking dish or 9-in. pie plate.

2 Bake, uncovered, at 350° for 20-25 minutes or until top is lightly browned. Sprinkle with tomatoes and onions. Serve with crackers or pita bread.

YIELD: 4½ CUPS.

EDITOR'S NOTE: Reduced-fat or fat-free mayonnaise is not recommended for this recipe.

Victoria Casey, Coeur d'Alene, Idaho

Green chilies add a bit of zip to this rich cracker spread. I serve it often at parties because it makes a lot, is quick to prepare and looks so pretty with the red tomatoes and green onions on top.

orange chocolate fondue

½ cup milk chocolate chips

3 squares (1 ounce *each*) bittersweet chocolate

½ cup heavy whipping cream

3 tablespoons orange juice concentrate

1 frozen pound cake (16 ounces), thawed and cut into 1-inch cubes

Sliced bananas and star fruit, orange segments, sweet cherries *or* strawberries *or* fruit of your choice

In a heavy saucepan, cook and stir the chocolate chips, bittersweet chocolate and cream over low heat until smooth. Stir in the orange juice concentrate. Transfer to a fondue pot and keep warm. Serve with cake and fruit.

YIELD: 1⅓ CUPS.

Mary Jean DeVries, Grandville, Michigan

Invite your family and friends to dip cubes of cake and pieces of fruit into this rich, luscious fondue for a special treat during the holiday season.

pesto cream cheese spread

1 package (8 ounces) cream cheese, softened

1/8 teaspoon garlic powder

1/3 cup grated Parmesan cheese

3 tablespoons butter, softened

1/2 cup minced fresh parsley

1 garlic clove, minced

1 teaspoon dried basil

1/2 teaspoon dried marjoram

1/4 cup finely chopped walnuts

3 tablespoons olive oil

Assorted crackers

1 Line a 5 3/4-in. x 3-in. x 2-in. loaf pan with plastic wrap. In a small mixing bowl, combine cream cheese and garlic powder until blended; set aside. In a bowl, combine Parmesan cheese, butter, parsley, garlic, basil and marjoram until blended. Stir in walnuts. Gradually stir in oil.

2 Spread about 1/4 cup cream cheese mixture in prepared pan. Carefully spread with a third of the Parmesan mixture. Repeat layers twice. Top with remaining cream cheese mixture. Cover and refrigerate for at least 5 hours. Unmold; serve with crackers.

YIELD: ABOUT 1 1/2 CUPS.

Cynthia Emshoff, Sarasota, Florida

This is a terrific appetizer to serve when hosting an Italian-themed meal. People may be a little hesitant to try it, but once they dip in, they won't be able to stop!

roasted goat cheese with garlic

6 to 8 garlic cloves, peeled

1 tablespoon vegetable oil

1 medium red onion, thinly sliced

2 tablespoons butter

1 tablespoon brown sugar

8 ounces crumbled goat *or* feta cheese

1 tablespoon white balsamic vinegar

Salt and pepper to taste

¼ cup thinly sliced fresh basil

Thinly sliced French bread *or* crackers

1 Place garlic and oil in a pie plate. Cover and bake at 350° for 30 minutes.

2 Meanwhile, in a skillet, saute onion in butter until tender and lightly browned. Add brown sugar; cook and stir until sugar is dissolved. Remove from the heat.

3 Remove garlic from pie plate. Spread onion in pie plate; top with cheese. Place garlic over cheese. Bake, uncovered, for 15-20 minutes or until cheese is melted.

4 Mash garlic with a fork. Stir vinegar, salt and pepper into garlic, onion and cheese mixture. Transfer to a serving bowl; sprinkle with basil. Serve warm with French bread or crackers.

YIELD: ABOUT 1¼ CUPS.

Carol Barlow, Berwyn, Illinois

Now that we have kids, my husband and I don't entertain much. But when we do, I serve this savory spread. The combination of goat cheese, garlic and onions always earns rave reviews.

hearty cheese spread

1 Gouda cheese round in red wax covering (7 ounces), room temperature

1 package (2½ ounces) thinly sliced smoked beef, finely chopped

¼ cup sour cream

2 tablespoons sweet pickle relish

2 teaspoons prepared horseradish

Apple slices *or* crackers

1 Carefully slice through wax and cheese to within 1 in. of the bottom, forming eight pie-shaped wedges. Carefully fold wax back to expose cheese; remove cheese.

2 In a mixing bowl, beat the cheese until creamy. Add the beef, sour cream, relish and horseradish; mix well. Spoon into wax shell. Chill.

3 Serve with apple slices or crackers.

YIELD: 1½ CUPS.

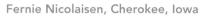

Fernie Nicolaisen, Cherokee, Iowa

Here's a cheese spread that will please a hungry crowd with its bold taste. Prepare this spread early in the day, spoon it into the wax shell and refrigerate until you are ready to serve.

guacamole dip

1 large ripe avocado, peeled

¼ cup plain yogurt

2 tablespoons picante sauce *or salsa*

1 tablespoon finely chopped onion

⅛ teaspoon salt

2 to 3 drops hot pepper sauce, optional

Tortilla chips

In a bowl, mash avocado until smooth. Stir in the yogurt, picante sauce, onion, salt and hot pepper sauce if desired. Cover and refrigerate until serving. Serve with tortilla chips.

YIELD: ¾ CUP.

Virginia Burwell, Dayton, Texas

Since guacamole is a favorite in this area with its emphasis on Mexican food, I decided to create my own recipe. I serve it as a dip for chips, with baked chicken or to top off a bed of lettuce.

all wrapped up

58

74

No fork or knife are required for these festive, finger foods! Delicious, savory fillings are packaged in an assortment of easy-to-find pastry doughs and wrappers. Your menu options range from Chorizo-Queso Egg Rolls (p. 53) and Southwestern Appetizer Triangles (p. 58) to Vegetable Spiral Sticks (p. 74).

For large gatherings, why not make a double batch? Then place one tray out and keep a second tray either in a warm oven or in the refrigerator, ready to go!

mushroom puffs

4 ounces cream cheese, cubed

1 can (4 ounces) mushroom stems and pieces, drained

1 tablespoon chopped onion

⅛ teaspoon hot pepper sauce

1 tube (8 ounces) crescent roll dough

1 In a blender or food processor, combine cream cheese, mushrooms, onion and hot pepper sauce; cover and process until blended. Unroll crescent dough; separate into four rectangles. Press perforations to seal. Spread mushroom mixture over dough.

2 Roll up jelly-roll style, starting with a long side. Cut each roll into five slices; place on an ungreased baking sheet. Bake at 425° for 8-10 minutes or until puffed and golden brown.

YIELD: 20 APPETIZERS.

Marilin Rosborough, Altoona, Pennsylvania
You can make these attractive appetizers in a jiffy with refrigerated crescent roll dough. The tasty little spirals disappear fast at a holiday party!

chicken salad cups

1 package (15 ounces) refrigerated pie pastry

2 cups diced cooked chicken

1 can (8 ounces) unsweetened crushed pineapple, drained

½ cup slivered almonds

½ cup chopped celery

½ cup shredded cheddar cheese

½ cup mayonnaise

½ teaspoon salt

½ teaspoon paprika

TOPPING:

½ cup sour cream

¼ cup mayonnaise

½ cup shredded cheddar cheese

1 Cut each sheet of pie pastry into 4½-in. rounds; reroll scraps and cut out additional circles. Press pastry onto the bottom and up the sides of 14 ungreased muffin cups. Bake at 450° for 6-7 minutes or until golden brown. Cool on a wire rack.

2 In a bowl, combine the chicken, pineapple, almonds, celery, cheese, mayonnaise, salt and paprika; refrigerate until chilled.

3 Just before serving, spoon two rounded tablespoonfuls of chicken salad into each pastry cup. Combine sour cream and mayonnaise; spoon over filling. Sprinkle with cheese.

YIELD: 14 SERVINGS.

Lois Holdson, Millersville, Maryland

Pineapple and almonds enhance the creamy chicken salad in these cute tartlets made with convenient refrigerated pie pastry.

mozzarella tomato tartlets

Amy Golden, East Aurora, New York

Convenient frozen phyllo shells add to this impressive appetizer's easy preparation. Although I make them year-round, they're especially tasty with garden-fresh tomatoes.

1 garlic clove, minced

1 tablespoon olive oil

1½ cups seeded chopped tomatoes

¾ cup shredded part-skim mozzarella cheese

½ teaspoon dried basil

Pepper to taste

24 frozen miniature phyllo tart shells

6 pitted ripe olives, quartered

Grated Parmesan cheese

1 In a small skillet, saute garlic in oil for 1 minute. Add the tomatoes; cook until liquid has evaporated. Remove from the heat; stir in the mozzarella cheese, basil and pepper.

2 Spoon 1 teaspoonful into each tart shell. Top each with a piece of olive; sprinkle with Parmesan cheese. Place on an ungreased baking sheet. Bake at 450° for 5-8 minutes or until bubbly.

YIELD: 2 DOZEN.

petite sausage quiches

1 cup butter, softened

2 packages (3 ounces *each*) cream cheese, softened

2 cups all-purpose flour

FILLING:

6 ounces bulk Italian sausage

1 cup (4 ounces) shredded Swiss cheese

1 tablespoon minced chives

2 eggs

1 cup half-and-half cream

¼ teaspoon salt

Dash cayenne pepper

1 In a mixing bowl, beat the butter, cream cheese and flour until smooth. Shape tablespoonfuls of dough into balls; press onto the bottom and up the sides of greased miniature muffin cups.

2 In a skillet, cook sausage over medium heat until no longer pink; drain. Sprinkle sausage, Swiss cheese and chives into muffin cups. In a bowl, beat eggs, cream, salt and pepper. Pour into shells.

3 Bake at 375° for 28-30 minutes or until browned. Serve warm.

YIELD: 3 DOZEN.

Dawn Stitt, Hesperia, Michigan

You won't be able to eat just one of these cute mini quiches. Filled with savory sausage, Swiss cheese and a dash of cayenne, the mouth-watering morsels will disappear fast from the breakfast or buffet table.

chorizo-queso egg rolls

½ cup mayonnaise

½ cup sour cream

2 ounces cream cheese, softened

2 tablespoons minced fresh cilantro

1 tablespoon chipotle peppers in adobo sauce

6 ounces uncooked chorizo *or* bulk spicy pork sausage

2 cups crumbled queso fresco

¼ cup enchilada sauce

¼ cup chopped green chilies

1 package (12 ounces) wonton wrappers

Oil for frying

1 For dipping sauce, in a small bowl, combine the mayonnaise, sour cream, cream cheese, cilantro and chipotle peppers. Cover and refrigerate until serving.

2 In a large skillet, cook chorizo over medium heat until no longer pink; drain. Stir in the queso fresco, enchilada sauce and chilies.

3 Position a wonton wrapper with one point toward you. Place 2 teaspoons of filling in the center. Fold bottom corner over filling; fold sides toward center over filling. Roll toward the remaining point. Moisten top corner with water; press to seal. Repeat with remaining wrappers and filling.

4 In an electric skillet, heat 1 in. of oil to 375°. Fry egg rolls in batches for 1-2 minutes on each side or until golden brown. Drain on paper towels. Serve warm with dipping sauce.

YIELD: 4 DOZEN.

EDITOR'S NOTE: Fill wonton wrappers a few at a time, keeping the others covered with a damp paper towel until ready to use.

Kari Wheaton, Beloit, Wisconsin

Little bites deliver big flavor in this combination of tangy sausage and creamy cheese in crisp wontons. The recipe is an appetizing take-off on my favorite Mexican entree.

asparagus ham spirals

8 fresh asparagus spears, trimmed

1 tube (8 ounces) refrigerated crescent rolls

1 carton (8 ounces) spreadable chive-and-onion cream cheese

4 thin rectangular slices deli ham

2 tablespoons butter, melted

¼ teaspoon garlic powder

1 Place asparagus in a skillet; add ½ in. of water. Bring to a boil. Reduced heat; cover and simmer for 3-5 minutes or until crisp-tender. Drain and set aside.

2 Separate crescent dough into four rectangles; seal perforations. Spread cream cheese over each rectangle to within ¼ in. of edges. Top each with ham, leaving ¼ in. uncovered on one long side. Place two asparagus spears along the long side with the ham; roll up and press seam to seal.

3 Cut each roll into seven pieces. Place cut side down 1 in. apart on greased baking sheets. Combine butter and garlic powder; brush over spirals. Bake at 375° for 10-12 minutes or until golden brown.

YIELD: 28 APPETIZERS.

Linda Fischer, Stuttgart, Arkansas

These appealing appetizers are sure to be a hit at your next party. I'm on the arts council in our small town, so I came up with this snack recipe to serve at some of the events we cater. People will think you really fussed with these yummy bites!

korean wontons

2 cups shredded cabbage

1 cup canned bean sprouts

1/2 cup shredded carrots

1 1/2 teaspoons plus 2 tablespoons vegetable oil, *divided*

1/3 pound ground beef

1/3 cup sliced green onions

1 1/2 teaspoons sesame seeds, toasted

1 1/2 teaspoons minced fresh gingerroot

3 garlic cloves, minced

1 1/2 teaspoons sesame oil

1/2 teaspoon salt

1/2 teaspoon pepper

1 package (12 ounces) wonton wrappers

1 egg, lightly beaten

3 tablespoons water

1 In a wok or large skillet, stir-fry cabbage, bean sprouts and carrots in 1 1/2 teaspoons oil until tender; set aside. In a skillet, cook beef over medium heat until no longer pink; drain. Add to vegetable mixture. Stir in onions, sesame seeds, ginger, garlic, sesame oil, salt and pepper.

2 Place about 1 tablespoon of filling in the center of each wonton wrapper. Combine egg and water. Moisten wonton edges with egg mixture; fold opposite corners over filling and press to seal. Heat remaining vegetable oil in a large skillet. Cook the wontons in batches for 1-2 minutes on each side or until golden brown, adding additional oil if needed.

YIELD: 5 DOZEN.

EDITOR'S NOTE: Fill wonton wrappers a few at a time, keeping the others covered with a damp paper towel until ready to use.

Christy Lee, Horsham, Pennsylvania

Korean wontons (mandoo) are not hot and spicy like many of the traditional Korean dishes. The fried dumplings, filled with vegetables and beef, are very easy to prepare, and the ingredients are inexpensive.

onion brie appetizers

2 medium onions, thinly sliced

3 tablespoons butter

2 tablespoons brown sugar

½ teaspoon white wine vinegar

1 sheet frozen puff pastry, thawed

4 ounces Brie *or* Camembert, rind removed, softened

1 to 2 teaspoons caraway seeds

1 egg

2 teaspoons water

1 In a large skillet, cook the onions, butter, brown sugar and vinegar over medium-low heat until onions are golden brown, stirring frequently. Remove with a slotted spoon; cool to room temperature.

2 On a lightly floured surface, roll puff pastry into an 11-in. x 8-in. rectangle. Spread Brie over pastry. Cover with the onions; sprinkle with caraway seeds.

3 Roll up one long side to the middle of the dough; roll up the other side so the two rolls meet in the center. Using a serrated knife, cut into ½-in. slices. Place on parchment paper-lined baking sheets; flatten to ¼-in. thickness. Refrigerate for 15 minutes.

4 In a small bowl, beat egg and water; brush over slices. Bake at 375° for 12-14 minutes or until puffed and golden brown. Serve warm.

YIELD: 1½ DOZEN.

Carole Resnick, Cleveland, Ohio

Guests will think you spent hours preparing these cute appetizers, but they're really easy to assemble, using purchased puff pastry. And the tasty combination of Brie, caramelized onions and caraway is terrific.

veggie wonton quiches

24 wonton wrappers

1 cup finely chopped fresh broccoli

¾ cup diced fresh mushrooms

½ cup diced sweet red pepper

¼ cup finely chopped onion

2 teaspoons vegetable oil

3 eggs

1 tablespoon water

2 teaspoons dried parsley flakes

¼ teaspoon salt

¼ teaspoon dried thyme

¼ teaspoon white pepper

Dash cayenne pepper

¾ cup shredded cheddar cheese

1 Gently press wonton wrappers into miniature muffin cups coated with nonstick cooking spray. Lightly coat wontons with nonstick cooking spray. Bake at 350° for 5 minutes. Remove wontons from cups; place upside down on baking sheets. Lightly coat with nonstick cooking spray. Bake 5 minutes longer or until light golden brown.

2 Meanwhile, in a nonstick skillet, cook the broccoli, mushrooms, red pepper and onion in oil over medium heat for 4-5 minutes or until crisp-tender. In a bowl, whisk eggs and water; stir in the parsley, salt, thyme, white pepper and cayenne. Add to vegetable mixture; cook over medium heat for 4-5 minutes or until eggs are completely set.

3 Remove from the heat; stir in cheese. Spoon about 1 tablespoonful into each wonton cup. Bake for 5 minutes or until filling is heated through. Serve warm.

YIELD: 2 DOZEN.

EDITOR'S NOTE: Fill wonton wrappers a few at a time, keeping the others covered with a damp paper towel until ready to use.

Taste of Home Test Kitchen

With green broccoli and red pepper, these mini quiches are a fitting finger food for Christmas. Crispy wonton cups make a fun crust.

southwestern appetizer triangles

Shelia Pope, Preston, Idaho

A nifty cross between egg rolls and tacos, these triangles are fun to serve, especially at the holidays. My mom created the recipe years ago, much to the delight of my family. Since I began making them, my husband insists we have them on Sundays during football season as well as for holiday celebrations.

1 pound ground beef

1 medium onion, chopped

Salt and pepper to taste

1 can (16 ounces) refried beans

1½ cups (6 ounces) shredded cheddar cheese

1 cup salsa

1 can (4 ounces) diced jalapeno peppers, drained

2 packages (12 ounces *each*) wonton wrappers

Oil for deep-fat frying

Additional salsa

1 In a skillet, cook the beef, onion, salt and pepper over medium heat until meat is no longer pink; drain. Add the beans, cheese, salsa and jalapenos. Cook and stir over low heat until the cheese is melted. Remove from the heat; cool for 10 minutes.

2 Place a teaspoonful of beef mixture in the center of one wonton wrapper. Moisten edges with water. Fold wontons in half, forming a triangle. Repeat.

3 In an electric skillet or deep-fat fryer, heat 1 in. of oil to 375°. Fry wontons, a few at a time, for 2-3 minutes or until golden brown. Drain on paper towels. Serve warm with salsa.

YIELD: ABOUT 7½ DOZEN.

EDITOR'S NOTE: Fill wonton wrappers a few at a time, keeping the others covered with a damp paper towel until ready to use.

mini sausage bundles

½ pound turkey Italian sausage links, casings removed

1 small onion, finely chopped

¼ cup finely chopped sweet red pepper

1 garlic clove, minced

½ cup shredded cheddar cheese

8 sheets phyllo dough (14 inches x 9 inches)

12 whole chives, optional

1 Crumble the sausage into a large nonstick skillet; add onion, red pepper and garlic. Cook over medium heat until meat is no longer pink; drain. Stir in cheese; cool slightly.

2 Place one sheet of phyllo dough on a work surface; coat with nonstick cooking spray. Cover with a second sheet of phyllo; coat with nonstick cooking spray. (Until ready to use, keep remaining phyllo covered with plastic wrap and a damp towel to prevent drying out.) Cut widthwise into three 4-in. strips, discarding trimmings. Top each with 2 rounded tablespoons of sausage mixture; fold bottom and side edges over the filling and roll up. Repeat with remaining phyllo and filling.

3 Place seam side down on an ungreased baking sheet. Bake at 425° for 5-6 minutes or until lightly browned. Tie a chive around each bundle if desired. Serve warm.

YIELD: 1 DOZEN.

Taste of Home Test Kitchen

These tasty hors d'oeuvres cut fat as well as cleanup by keeping the deep fryer at bay. The savory bundles are filled with turkey sausage, garlic and onion.

sausage biscuit bites

1 tube (7½ ounces) refrigerated buttermilk biscuits

1 tablespoon butter, melted

4½ teaspoons grated Parmesan cheese

1 teaspoon dried oregano

1 package (8 ounces) brown-and-serve sausage links

1 On a lightly floured surface, roll out each biscuit into a 4-in. circle; brush with butter. Combine Parmesan cheese and oregano; sprinkle over butter. Place a sausage link in the center of each roll; roll up.

2 Cut each widthwise into four pieces; insert a toothpick into each. Place on an ungreased baking sheet. Bake at 375° for 8-10 minutes or until golden brown.

YIELD: 40 APPETIZERS.

Audrey Marler, Kokomo, Indiana

I sometimes bake these delightful little morsels the night before, refrigerate them, then put them in the slow cooker in the morning so my husband can share them with his co-workers. They're always gone in a hurry.

mozzarella puffs

1 tube (7½ ounces) refrigerated buttermilk biscuits

1 teaspoon dried oregano

1 block (2 to 3 ounces) mozzarella cheese

2 tablespoons pizza sauce

Make an indentation in the center of each biscuit; sprinkle with oregano. Cut the mozzarella into 10 cubes, ¾-in. each; place a cube in the center of each biscuit. Pinch dough tightly around cheese to seal. Place seam side down on an ungreased baking sheet. Spread pizza sauce over tops. Bake at 375° for 10-12 minutes or until golden brown. Serve warm. Refrigerate leftovers.

YIELD: 10 SERVINGS.

Joan Mousley Dziuba, Waupaca, Wisconsin

These savory cheesy biscuits go over great at my house. Since they're so quick to make, I can whip up a batch anytime.

chili cheese snacks

2 packages (3 ounces *each*) cream cheese, softened

1 cup (4 ounces) shredded cheddar cheese

¼ cup chopped green chilies

¼ cup chopped ripe olives, drained

2 teaspoons dried minced onion

¼ teaspoon hot pepper sauce

2 tubes (8 ounces *each*) refrigerated crescent rolls

1 In a small mixing bowl, beat cream cheese. Add the cheddar cheese, chilies, olives, onion and hot pepper sauce. Separate each tube of crescent dough into four rectangles; press perforations to seal.

2 Spread cheese mixture over dough. Roll up jelly-roll style, starting with a long side. Cut each roll into 10 slices; place on greased baking sheets. Bake at 400° for 8-10 minutes or until golden brown.

YIELD: 80 APPETIZERS.

Carol Nelson, Cool, California

I've been collecting appetizer recipes for more than 20 years and have a host of tasty treats. These handheld morsels are perfect for parties because they allow folks to walk around and mingle.

artichoke wonton cups

1 cup grated Parmesan cheese

1 cup mayonnaise

½ teaspoon onion powder

½ teaspoon garlic powder

2 cups (8 ounces) shredded part-skim mozzarella cheese

1 can (14 ounces) water-packed artichoke hearts, rinsed, drained and chopped

1 package (12 ounces) wonton wrappers

1 In a small mixing bowl, combine the Parmesan cheese, mayonnaise, onion powder and garlic powder; mix well. Stir in the mozzarella cheese and artichokes; set aside.

2 Coat one side of each wonton wrapper with nonstick cooking spray; press greased side down into miniature muffin cups. Bake at 350° for 5 minutes or until edges are lightly browned.

3 Fill each cup with 1 tablespoon artichoke mixture. Bake 5-6 minutes longer or until golden brown. Serve warm.

YIELD: ABOUT 4 DOZEN.

Paige Scott, Murfreesboro, Tennessee

I came up with this recipe by combining several artichoke dip recipes. Wonton cups add a fancy look that's perfect for special occasions. If you're serving a large crowd, you may want to double the recipe.

sausage breadsticks

1 tube (11 ounces) refrigerated breadstick dough

8 smoked sausage links *or* hot dogs

1 Separate the dough into eight strips; unroll and wrap one strip around each sausage. Place on an ungreased baking sheet.

2 Bake at 350° for 15-17 minutes or until golden brown. Serve warm.

YIELD: 4 SERVINGS.

Taste of Home Test Kitchen

Bring out the kid in everyone by preparing these snacks. This old-fashioned finger food is a fun addition to a breakfast buffet.

ham and cheese tarts

2 packages (3 ounces *each*) cream cheese, softened

½ cup French onion dip

1 tablespoon milk

¼ teaspoon ground mustard

¼ teaspoon grated orange peel

½ cup finely chopped fully cooked ham

1 tube (12 ounces) refrigerated buttermilk biscuits

¼ teaspoon paprika

1 In a small mixing bowl, beat the cream cheese, onion dip, milk, mustard and orange peel until blended. Stir in ham.

2 Split each biscuit into thirds; press into lightly greased miniature muffin cups. Spoon a scant tablespoonful of the ham mixture into each cup; sprinkle with paprika. Bake at 375° for 12-17 minutes or until golden brown. Serve warm.

YIELD: 2½ DOZEN.

Delores Romyn, Stratton, Ontario

These savory tarts have been a family favorite for years. Make the ham mixture in advance to save time when guests arrive.

pizza rolls

4 cups (16 ounces) shredded pizza cheese blend *or* part-skim mozzarella cheese

1 pound bulk Italian sausage, cooked and drained

2 packages (3 ounces *each*) sliced pepperoni, chopped

1 medium green pepper, finely chopped

1 medium sweet red pepper, finely chopped

1 medium onion, finely chopped

2 jars (14 ounces *each*) pizza sauce

32 egg roll wrappers

Oil for frying

Additional pizza sauce for dipping, warmed, optional

1 In a large bowl, combine the cheese, sausage, pepperoni, peppers and onion. Stir in pizza sauce until combined. Place about 1/4 cup filling in the center of each egg roll wrapper. (Keep wrappers covered with a damp paper towel until ready to use.) Fold bottom corner over filling; fold sides toward center over filling. Moisten remaining corner with water and roll up tightly to seal.

2 In an electric skillet, heat 1 in. of oil to 375°. Fry pizza rolls for 1-2 minutes on each side or until golden brown. Drain on paper towels. Serve with additional pizza sauce if desired.

YIELD: 32 ROLLS.

Julie Gaines, Normal, Illinois

This is my husband's version of store-bought pizza rolls, and our family loves them. Although they take some time to make, they freeze well. So when we're through, we get to enjoy the fruits of our labor for a long time!

veggie shrimp egg rolls

Carole Resnick, Cleveland, Ohio

These wonderful appetizers will be the hit of your next party. They're versatile in that you can also used cooked crab, lobster or chicken.

2 teaspoons minced fresh gingerroot

1 garlic clove, minced

3 tablespoons olive oil, *divided*

½ pound uncooked medium shrimp, peeled, deveined and chopped

2 green onions, finely chopped

1 medium carrot, finely chopped

1 medium sweet red pepper, finely chopped

1 cup canned bean sprouts, rinsed and finely chopped

2 tablespoons water

2 tablespoons reduced-sodium soy sauce

38 wonton wrappers

DIPPING SAUCE:

¾ cup apricot spreadable fruit

1 tablespoon water

1 tablespoon lime juice

1 tablespoon reduced-sodium soy sauce

1½ teaspoons Dijon mustard

¼ teaspoon minced fresh gingerroot

1 In a large skillet, saute ginger and garlic in 1 tablespoon oil over medium heat until tender. Add the shrimp, onions, carrot, red pepper, bean sprouts, water and soy sauce; cook and stir for 2-3 minutes or vegetables are crisp-tender and shrimp turn pink. Reduce heat to low; cook for 4-5 minutes or until most of the liquid has evaporated. Remove from the heat; let stand for 15 minutes.

2 Place a tablespoonful of shrimp mixture in the center of a wonton wrapper. (Keep wrappers covered with a damp paper towel until ready to use.) Fold bottom corner over filling. Fold sides toward center over filling. Moisten remaining corner with water; roll up tightly to seal.

3 In a large skillet over medium heat, cook egg rolls, a few at a time, in remaining oil for 5-7 minutes on each side or until golden brown. Drain on paper towels.

4 In a blender or food processor, combine the sauce ingredients; cover and process until smooth. Serve with egg rolls.

YIELD: 38 EGG ROLLS.

gouda bites

1 tube (8 ounces) refrigerated reduced-fat crescent rolls

½ teaspoon garlic powder

5 ounces Gouda cheese, cut into 24 pieces

1 Unroll crescent dough into one long rectangle; seal the seams and perforations. Sprinkle with garlic powder. Cut into 24 pieces; lightly press onto the bottom and up the sides of ungreased miniature muffin cups.

2 Bake at 375° for 3 minutes. Place a piece of the cheese in each cup. Bake 8-10 minutes longer or until golden brown and cheese is melted. Serve warm.

YIELD: 2 DOZEN.

Phylis Behringer, Defiance, Ohio

I season refrigerated dough with garlic powder to create these golden cheese-filled cups.

olive-cheese nuggets

2 cups (8 ounces) shredded cheddar
  cheese

1¼ cups all-purpose flour

½ cup butter, melted

½ teaspoon paprika

36 pimiento-stuffed olives

1 In a small mixing bowl, beat cheese, flour, butter and paprika until
  blended. Pat olives dry; shape 1 teaspoon of cheese mixture around
  each.

2 Place 2 in. apart on ungreased baking sheets. Bake at 400° for 12-15
  minutes or until golden brown.

YIELD: 3 DOZEN.

Lavonne Hartel, Williston, North Dakota

More than 20 years ago, I tried these olive-stuffed treats for a holiday party.

Friends are still asking me to bring them to get-togethers.

chili cheese tart

1 package (15 ounces) refrigerated
  pie pastry (2 sheets)

1 can (4 ounces) chopped green
  chilies, drained

1 cup (4 ounces) shredded cheddar
  cheese

1 cup (4 ounces) shredded Monterey
  Jack cheese

¼ teaspoon chili powder

Salsa and sour cream

1 Place one sheet of pie pastry on an ungreased pizza pan or baking
  sheet. Sprinkle chilies and cheeses over pastry to within ½ in. of
  edges. Top with remaining pastry; seal edges and prick top with a fork.

2 Sprinkle with chili powder. Bake at 450° for 10-15 minutes or until
  golden brown. Cool for 10 minutes before cutting into wedges. Serve
  with salsa and sour cream.

YIELD: 10-14 SERVINGS.

Rachel Nash, Pascagoula, Mississippi

When I fix this flavorful appetizer, I have to keep an eye out for sneaky fingers.

My family just can't resist sampling the cheesy wedges.

pizza turnovers

- 3 tablespoons chopped fresh mushrooms
- 2 tablespoons chopped green pepper
- 2 tablespoons chopped onion
- 1 tablespoon butter
- 5 tablespoons tomato paste
- 2 tablespoons water
- 1/2 teaspoon dried oregano
- 1/8 teaspoon garlic powder
- 1/2 cup shredded part-skim mozzarella cheese
- 1 package (15 ounces) refrigerated pie pastry
- 1 egg, lightly beaten

1 In a small saucepan, saute the mushrooms, green pepper and onion in butter until tender. Add the tomato paste, water, oregano and garlic powder. Reduce heat to medium-low. Stir in cheese until melted. Remove from the heat.

2 Cut 3 1/2-in. circles from pie pastry. Place 1 teaspoon filling in the center of each circle. Brush edges of dough with water. Fold each circle in half; seal edges with a fork. Brush the tops with beaten egg. Place the turnovers on a greased baking sheet.

3 Bake at 425° for 12-14 minutes or until golden brown.

YIELD: 14 TURNOVERS.

EDITOR'S NOTE: The turnovers may be frozen, unbaked, for up to 2 months. Before serving, bake at 425° for 16-18 minutes or until golden brown and heated through.

Janet Crouch, Three Hills, Alberta
These little pizza snacks are a real crowd-pleaser. Plus they can be made ahead and frozen, so you don't have to worry about last-minute preparation.

bite-size crab quiches

1 tube (16.3 ounces) large
  refrigerated buttermilk biscuits

1 can (6 ounces) crabmeat, drained,
  flaked and cartilage removed *or*
  1 cup chopped imitation crabmeat

½ cup shredded Swiss cheese

1 egg

½ cup milk

½ teaspoon dill weed

¼ teaspoon salt

1 Separate each biscuit into five equal pieces. Press onto the bottom and up the sides of 24 ungreased miniature muffin cups (discard remaining piece of dough). Fill each cup with 2 teaspoons crab and 1 teaspoon Swiss cheese. In a small bowl, combine the egg, milk, dill and salt; spoon about 1½ teaspoons into each cup.

2 Bake at 375° for 15-20 minutes or until edges are golden brown. Let stand for 5 minutes before removing from pans. Serve warm.

YIELD: 2 DOZEN.

Virginia Ricks, Roy, Utah

These mouth-watering morsels make an appealing appetizer when you invite a few friends to the house after a movie or ball game.

creamy herb appetizer pockets

1 carton (4.4 ounces) reduced-fat garlic-herb cheese spread

4 ounces reduced-fat cream cheese

2 tablespoons half-and-half cream

1 garlic clove, minced

1 tablespoon dried basil

1 teaspoon dried thyme

1/2 teaspoon celery salt

1/4 teaspoon dill weed

1/4 teaspoon salt

1/4 teaspoon pepper

3 to 4 drops hot pepper sauce

1/2 cup chopped canned water-packed artichoke hearts

1/4 cup chopped roasted red peppers

2 tubes (8 ounces *each*) refrigerated reduced-fat crescent rolls

1 In a small mixing bowl, beat the cheese spread, cream cheese, cream and garlic until blended. Beat in the herbs, salt, pepper and hot pepper sauce. Fold in artichokes and red peppers. Cover and chill for at least 1 hour.

2 Unroll both tubes of crescent roll dough. On a lightly floured surface, form each tube of dough into a long rectangle; seal the seams and perforations. Roll each into a 16-in. x 12-in. rectangle. Cut lengthwise into four strips and widthwise into three strips; separate squares.

3 Place 1 rounded tablespoon of filling in the center of each square. Fold in half, forming triangles. Crimp edges to seal; trim if necessary. Place on ungreased baking sheets. Bake at 375° for 10-15 minutes or until golden brown. Serve warm.

YIELD: 2 DOZEN.

EDITOR'S NOTE: This recipe was tested with Bourisn Light Cheese Spread with garlic and fine herbs. One carton contains about 7 tablespoons of cheese spread.

Tina Scarpaci, Chandler, Arizona

I combined a creamy cheese sauce and an artichoke dip to come up with these bite-size morsels. The filling is tucked into triangles made from crescent roll dough— it's the perfect no-mess appetizer!

party pesto pinwheels

- 1 tube (8 ounces) refrigerated crescent rolls
- 1/3 cup prepared pesto sauce
- 1/4 cup roasted sweet red peppers, drained and chopped
- 1/4 cup grated Parmesan cheese
- 1 cup pizza sauce, warmed

1 Unroll crescent dough into two long rectangles; seal seams and perforations. Spread each with pesto; sprinkle with red peppers and Parmesan cheese.

2 Roll each up jelly-roll style, starting with a short side. With a sharp knife, cut each roll into 10 slices. Place cut side down 2 in. apart on two ungreased baking sheets.

3 Bake at 400° for 8-10 minutes or until golden brown. Serve warm with pizza sauce.

YIELD: 20 SERVINGS.

Kathleen Farrell, Rochester, New York

I took a couple of my favorite recipes and combined them into these delicious hors d'oeuvres. These easy-to-make snacks are impressive.

vegetable spiral sticks

Teri Albrecht, Mt. Airy, Maryland

I love to serve these savory wrapped vegetable sticks for parties or special occasions. They're a simple but impressive appetizer.

3 medium carrots

12 fresh asparagus spears, trimmed

1 tube (11 ounces) refrigerated breadsticks

1 egg white, beaten

1/4 cup grated Parmesan cheese

1/2 teaspoon dried oregano

1 Cut carrots lengthwise into quarters. In a large skillet, bring 2 in. of water to a boil. Add carrots; cook for 3 minutes. Add asparagus; cook 2-3 minutes longer. Drain and rinse with cold water; pat dry.

2 Cut each piece of breadstick dough in half. Roll each piece into a 7-in. rope. Wrap one rope in a spiral around each vegetable. Place on a baking sheet coated with nonstick cooking spray; tuck ends of dough under vegetables to secure.

3 Brush with egg white. Combine Parmesan cheese and oregano; sprinkle over sticks. Bake at 375° for 12-14 minutes or until golden brown. Serve warm.

YIELD: 2 DOZEN.

crispy crab rangoon

1 package (3 ounces) cream cheese, softened

2 green onions, finely chopped

¼ cup finely chopped imitation crabmeat

1 teaspoon minced garlic

16 wonton wrappers

Oil for frying

Sweet-and-sour sauce

1 In a small mixing bowl, beat cream cheese until smooth. Add the onions, crab and garlic; mix well.

2 Place about 1½ teaspoons in the center of each wonton wrapper. Moisten edges with water; fold opposite corners over filling and press to seal.

3 In an electric skillet, heat 1 in. of oil to 375°. Fry wontons for 1-2 minutes or until golden brown, turning once. Drain on paper towels. Serve with sweet-and-sour sauce.

YIELD: 16 APPETIZERS.

EDITOR'S NOTE: Fill wonton wrappers a few at a time, keeping the others covered with a damp paper towel until ready to use.

Cathy Blankman, Warroad, Minnesota

My husband loved the appetizers we ordered at a Chinese restaurant so much that I was determined to make them at home. After two more trips to the restaurant to taste them again and about four home trials, I had them perfected. I often make the filling earlier in the day to save time later.

mini bacon quiches

1 package (15 ounces) refrigerated pie pastry

½ pound sliced bacon, cooked and crumbled

½ cup ricotta cheese

½ cup shredded cheddar cheese

½ cup shredded part-skim mozzarella cheese

1 egg, lightly beaten

1 small onion, finely chopped

¼ teaspoon garlic powder

⅛ teaspoon salt

Dash pepper

Dash cayenne pepper

2 teaspoons all-purpose flour

1 Let pastry stand at room temperature for 15-20 minutes.

2 In a bowl, combine the bacon, cheeses, egg, onion, garlic powder, salt, pepper and cayenne.

3 Sprinkle each pastry crust with 1 teaspoon flour; place floured side down on a lightly floured surface. Cut 12 circles from each crust, using a 2½-in. round biscuit cutter.

4 Press dough onto the bottom and up the sides of lightly greased miniature muffin cups. Fill each with about 1 tablespoon of bacon mixture. Bake at 400° for 16-18 minutes or until filling is set. Cool for 5 minutes before removing from pans to a wire rack. Serve warm.

YIELD: 2 DOZEN.

Julie Nowakowski, LaSalle, Illinois

Brimming with bacon and cheese, these melt-in-your-mouth tidbits are easy for guests to handle, and they look so colorful on a buffet. Nobody can stop with just one.

spinach phyllo bundles

1 medium onion, chopped

2 tablespoons plus ½ cup butter, *divided*

1 package (10 ounces) frozen chopped spinach, thawed and squeezed dry

1 cup (4 ounces) crumbled feta cheese

¾ cup small-curd cottage cheese

3 eggs, lightly beaten

¼ cup dry bread crumbs

¾ teaspoon salt

½ teaspoon dill weed

Pepper to taste

20 sheets phyllo dough (14-inch x 9-inch sheet size)

1 In a large skillet, saute onion in 2 tablespoons butter until tender. Remove from the heat. Stir in the spinach, feta cheese, cottage cheese, eggs, bread crumbs, salt, dill and pepper.

2 Melt remaining butter. Layer and brush five phyllo sheets with melted butter. (Keep remaining phyllo dough covered with plastic wrap and a damp towel to prevent it from drying out.) Cut the buttered sheets lengthwise into 2-in. strips. Place 1 heaping tablespoon of filling at one end of each strip; fold into a triangle, as you would fold a flag. Place on an ungreased baking sheet. Brush with butter. Repeat three times, using five sheets of phyllo each time.

3 Bake at 400° for 15-20 minutes or until golden brown. Serve warm.

YIELD: 28 APPETIZERS.

Eloise Olive, Greensboro, North Carolina
These crispy, golden triangles were inspired by spanakopita, a Greek spinach pie made with phyllo dough. The snacks are always winners.

empanditas

½ pound boneless skinless chicken breast halves, thinly sliced

1 tablespoon vegetable oil

⅛ teaspoon ground cumin

1 can (4 ounces) chopped green chilies, drained

½ cup shredded pepper Jack cheese *or* Monterey Jack cheese

2 tablespoons all-purpose flour

Pastry for 2 double-crust pies

¼ cup milk

1 In a large skillet, saute chicken in oil for 7-8 minutes or until juices run clear. Sprinkle with cumin. Chop into very small pieces and place in a bowl. Add chilies and cheese. Sprinkle with flour; toss to coat.

2 Turn pastry dough onto a floured surface; roll to ⅛-in. thickness. Cut with a 2-in. round cutter. Fill each circle with about 1 tablespoon of filling. Wet edges of circle with water. Fold half of pastry over filling; seal with fingers, then press with the tines of a fork. Repeat until all filling is used.

3 Place on a greased baking sheet. Brush lightly with milk. Bake at 375° for 20-25 minutes or until golden brown. Serve warm.

YIELD: 3 DOZEN.

EDITOR'S NOTE: Empanditas may be frozen after sealing. Brush with milk and bake for 30-35 minutes.

Mary Ann Kosmas, Minneapolis, Minnesota

These mini chicken pockets are one of my favorite appetizers because they can be made ahead of time and frozen. So they're a perfect snack when unexpected company drops in.

handheld snacks

84

106

When the gang is hungry, surprise them with these pizzas and sandwiches. This fare is more substantial... and is great for game nights or after-school snacks. Check out all the delicious options from Italian Subs (p. 91) and Spicy Summer Sub (p. 84) to Double Sausage Pizza (p. 106).

These snacks are ideal for portion control, too! When offering a variety of foods, cut these into smaller pieces for just a taste. Or, serve larger pieces when they are your main menu attraction.

turkey tortilla spirals

¾ pound thinly sliced deli turkey

6 flour tortillas (8 inches)

1 package (8 ounces) fat-free cream cheese

6 tablespoons finely chopped pecans

1 can (16 ounces) whole-berry cranberry sauce, *divided*

¼ cup chopped celery

2 green onions, thinly sliced

1 | Place turkey on tortillas to within ¼ in. of edge. Spread cream cheese over turkey; sprinkle with pecans. Spread each with 2 tablespoons cranberry sauce. Roll up jelly-roll style; wrap tightly in plastic wrap. Refrigerate for 1 hour or until firm.

2 | Just before serving, cut each roll into six pieces. In a small bowl, combine the celery, onions and remaining cranberry sauce. Serve with tortilla spirals.

YIELD: 3 DOZEN.

Peggy Grieme, Pinehurst, North Carolina

No one suspects that these addictive pinwheels are light. People are always surprised by how easy they are to make.

southwestern chicken pizza

1 medium onion, julienned

1 medium green pepper, julienned

¼ cup water

1 tube (10 ounces) refrigerated pizza crust

1¼ cups salsa

2 packages (6 ounces *each*) ready-to-use Southwestern chicken strips

2 cups (8 ounces) shredded Mexican cheese blend

¼ teaspoon garlic powder

¼ teaspoon dried cilantro flakes

1 In a microwave-safe bowl, combine the onion, green pepper and water. Cover and microwave on high for 2-4 minutes or until vegetables are crisp-tender; drain well.

2 Unroll pizza crust onto a greased baking sheet, stretching gently to form a 14-in. x 10-in. rectangle. Spread with salsa. Top with chicken and onion mixture. Sprinkle with cheese, garlic powder and cilantro. Bake at 400° for 15-20 minutes or until crust is golden and cheese is melted. Cut into squares.

YIELD: 8 SLICES.

EDITOR'S NOTE: This recipe was tested in a 1,100-watt microwave.

Robin Poust, Stevensville, Maryland

Our family loves Mexican food and pizza, so I combined the two. It's easy to cook the pepper and onion in the microwave. Salsa, prepared chicken and other convenience items hurry along the rest of the recipe. The final result is fantastic!

spicy summer sub

Barb McMahan, Fenton, Missouri

A few years back, I served this sandwich to friends and family who came to help with our garage sale. Everyone was impressed with the preparation and combination of flavors.

1 round loaf (1½ pounds) rye bread

1 cup mayonnaise

2 tablespoons Dijon mustard

1 jar (2 ounces) diced pimientos, drained

¼ to ½ teaspoon hot pepper sauce

½ pound sliced provolone cheese

¼ pound sliced fully cooked ham

¼ pound sliced Genoa salami

¼ pound sliced cooked turkey

¼ pound sliced mozzarella cheese

1 Cut bread in half horizontally; hollow out top and bottom, leaving a ¾-in. shell. (Discard removed bread or save for another use.)

2 In a small bowl, combine the mayonnaise, mustard, pimientos and hot pepper sauce; spread ¼ cup in the bottom bread shell. Layer with a fourth of the provolone, ham, turkey, salami and mozzarella. Spread with more of the mayonnaise mixture. Repeat layers three times (you may not use up all of the mayonnaise mixture). Replace bread top and wrap tightly with plastic wrap. Chill for at least 3 hours.

3 Remove from the refrigerator 30 minutes before serving. Cut into wedges; serve with remaining mayonnaise mixture if desired.

YIELD: 6-8 SERVINGS.

tomato rosemary focaccia

1 tube (13.8 ounces) refrigerated pizza crust

2 tablespoons olive oil

2 garlic cloves, minced

¼ teaspoon salt

1 tablespoon minced fresh rosemary *or* 1 teaspoon dried rosemary, crushed, *divided*

2 to 3 plum tomatoes, thinly sliced

1 small red onion, thinly sliced

Unroll pizza crust onto a greased baking sheet. Combine the oil, garlic, salt and half of the rosemary; spread over crust. Top with tomatoes and onion; sprinkle with remaining rosemary. Bake at 425° for 12-15 minutes or until golden. Cut into rectangles.

YIELD: 6 SERVINGS.

Dorothy Smith, El Dorado, Arkansas

This quick Italian flat bread is a delicious savory snack and is also good with soup or a salad.

turkey roll-ups

1 package (8 ounces) fat-free cream cheese

½ cup reduced-fat mayonnaise

¼ teaspoon dried basil

¼ teaspoon dried oregano

¼ teaspoon dill weed

¼ teaspoon garlic powder

10 flour tortillas (6 inches), warmed

1 medium onion, chopped

10 slices deli turkey breast (1 ounce *each*)

Shredded lettuce

In a small mixing bowl, combine the first six ingredients; beat until smooth. Spread over the tortillas. Sprinkle with onion; top with turkey and lettuce. Roll up tightly jelly-roll style; serve immediately.

YIELD: 10 SERVINGS.

Paula Alf, Cincinnati, Ohio

Whether served whole for lunch or cut into bite-size appetizers, these light wraps are always a hit. We prefer this blend of herbs, but feel free to use any combination you'd like.

party pitas

1 package (8 ounces) cream cheese, softened

½ cup mayonnaise

½ teaspoon dill weed

¼ teaspoon garlic salt

8 mini pita breads (4 inches)

16 fresh spinach leaves

¾ pound shaved fully cooked ham

½ pound thinly sliced Monterey Jack cheese

1 In a large mixing bowl, beat the cream cheese, mayonnaise, dill and garlic salt until blended.

2 Cut each pita in half horizontally; spread 1 tablespoon cream cheese mixture on each cut surface. On eight pita halves, layer spinach, ham and cheese. Top with remaining pita halves. Cut each pita into four wedges; secure with a toothpick.

YIELD: 32 PIECES.

Janette Root, Ellensburg, Washington

Whenever the ladies of our church host a bridal shower, these pita sandwiches are on the menu. Not only are they easy and delicious, they look nice on the table.

mediterranean pizza

2 jars (6½ ounces *each*) marinated artichoke hearts

1 loaf (1 pound) frozen bread dough, thawed

1 teaspoon dried basil

1 teaspoon dried oregano

½ teaspoon dried thyme

2 cups (8 ounces) shredded Monterey Jack cheese, *divided*

¼ pound thinly sliced deli ham, julienned

1 cup halved cherry tomatoes

1 cup chopped ripe olives

¼ cup crumbled feta cheese

1 Drain artichokes, reserving marinade. Chop artichokes; set aside. On a floured surface, roll bread dough into a 15-in. circle. Transfer to a greased 14-in. pizza pan; build up edges slightly. Brush the dough lightly with reserved marinade.

2 Combine the basil, oregano and thyme; sprinkle over marinade. Sprinkle with 1 cup Monterey Jack cheese, ham, artichokes, tomatoes, olives and feta cheese. Sprinkle with remaining Monterey Jack cheese. Bake at 400° for 20-25 minutes or until crust and cheese are lightly browned.

YIELD: 4-6 SERVINGS.

Pamela Brooks, South Berwick, Maine
Tangy marinated artichokes add flavor to both the crust and the topping of this delicious specialty pizza.

reuben roll-ups

1 tube (13.8 ounces) refrigerated pizza crust

1 cup sauerkraut, well drained

1 tablespoon Thousand Island salad dressing

4 slices corned beef, halved

4 slices Swiss cheese, halved

1 Roll dough into a 12-in. x 9-in. rectangle. Cut into eight 3-in. x 4½-in. rectangles. Combine sauerkraut and salad dressing. Place a slice of beef on each rectangle. Top with about 2 tablespoons sauerkraut mixture and a slice of cheese. Roll up.

2 Place with seam side down on a greased baking sheet. Bake at 425° for 12-14 minutes or until golden.

YIELD: 8 ROLL-UPS.

Patty Kile, Greentown, Pennsylvania
This recipe turns the popular Reuben sandwich into an interesting and hearty snack. We love these roll-ups at our house.

sausage pizza loaf

- 1 pound bulk Italian sausage
- 1/4 cup *each* chopped onion, sweet red pepper and green pepper
- 2 packages (6 1/2 ounces *each*) pizza crust mix
- 1 cup (4 ounces) shredded part-skim mozzarella cheese
- 1/2 cup chopped pepperoni
- 1 egg, lightly beaten
- 2 tablespoons grated Parmesan cheese
- 1 teaspoon dried oregano
- 1/4 teaspoon garlic powder

1 In a large skillet, cook the sausage, onion and peppers over medium heat until the meat is no longer pink; drain. Combine crust mixes; prepare according to package directions. With greased fingers, press onto the bottom of a greased 15-in. x 10-in. x 1-in. baking pan.

2 Combine the sausage mixture, mozzarella cheese, pepperoni and egg; spread over dough to within 1/2 in. of the edges. Sprinkle with the Parmesan cheese, oregano and garlic powder.

3 Roll up jelly-roll style, starting with a long side; pinch seams to seal. Arrange seam side down on pan and shape into a crescent. Bake at 400° for 30 minutes or until golden brown.

YIELD: 15 SERVINGS.

Pat Coon, Ulster, Pennsylvania

Savory slices of this bread make a popular Saturday night meal for my family. Just like pizza, it can be eaten as a fun finger food. Guests can't stop nibbling when I serve it at parties. Plus, it's good warm or cold.

italian subs

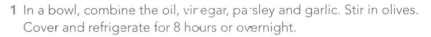

1/3 cup olive oil

4 1/2 teaspoons white wine vinegar

1 tablespoon dried parsley flakes

2 to 3 garlic cloves, minced

1 can (2 1/4 ounces) sliced ripe olives, drained

1/2 cup chopped stuffed olives

1 loaf (1 pound, 20 inches) French bread, unsliced

24 thin slices hard salami

24 slices provolone cheese

24 slices fully cooked ham

Lettuce leaves, optional

1 In a bowl, combine the oil, vinegar, parsley and garlic. Stir in olives. Cover and refrigerate for 8 hours or overnight.

2 Cut bread in half lengthwise. Place olive mixture on the bottom of bread. Top with the salami, cheese and ham; add lettuce if desired. Replace top. Cut into 2-in. slices. Insert a toothpick in each slice.

YIELD: 10 SERVINGS.

Delores Christner, Spooner, Wisconsin

Olive lovers are sure to rejoice over this stacked sandwich! Stuffed and ripe olives are marinated in white wine vinegar and garlic before using them to flavor these speedy salami, ham and provolone subs.

chicago-style pan pizza

Nikki MacDonald, Sheboygan, Wisconsin

I developed a love for Chicago's deep-dish pizzas while attending college in the Windy City. This simple recipe relies on frozen bread dough, so I can indulge in the mouth-watering sensation without leaving home.

1 loaf (1 pound) frozen bread dough, thawed

1 pound bulk Italian sausage

2 cups (8 ounces) shredded part-skim mozzarella cheese

½ pound sliced fresh mushrooms

1 small onion, chopped

2 teaspoons olive oil

1 can (28 ounces) diced tomatoes, drained

¾ teaspoon dried oregano

½ teaspoon salt

½ teaspoon fennel seed, crushed

¼ teaspoon garlic powder

½ cup grated Parmesan cheese

1 Press dough onto the bottom and up the sides of a greased 13-in. x 9-in. x 2-in. baking dish. In a large skillet, cook sausage over medium heat until no longer pink; drain. Sprinkle over dough. Top with mozzarella cheese.

2 In a skillet, saute mushrooms and onion in oil until onion is tender. Stir in the tomatoes, oregano, salt, fennel seed and garlic powder. Spoon over mozzarella cheese. Sprinkle with Parmesan cheese. Bake at 350° for 25-35 minutes or until crust is golden brown.

YIELD: 6 SLICES.

curried chicken tea sandwiches

2 cups cubed cooked chicken

1 medium unpeeled red apple, chopped

¾ cup dried cranberries

½ cup thinly sliced celery

¼ cup chopped pecans

2 tablespoons thinly sliced green onions

¾ cup mayonnaise

2 teaspoons lime juice

½ to ¾ teaspoon curry powder

12 slices bread

Lettuce leaves

1 In a bowl, combine the first six ingredients. Combine mayonnaise, lime juice and curry powder; add to chicken mixture and stir to coat. Cover and refrigerate until ready to serve.

2 Cut each slice of bread with a 3-in. heart-shaped cookie cutter if desired. Top with lettuce and chicken salad.

YIELD: 6 SERVINGS.

Robin Fuhrman, Fond du Lac, Wisconsin

At the Victorian-theme bridal shower I hosted, I spread this dressed-up chicken salad on bread triangles. Apples and dried cranberries add color and tang.

tree and star crab sandwiches

¾ cup mayonnaise

¾ cup shredded sharp cheddar cheese

1 can (6 ounces) crabmeat, drained, flaked and cartilage removed

2 tablespoons prepared French salad dressing

½ teaspoon prepared horseradish

Dash hot pepper sauce

48 bread slices

Fresh dill sprigs

In a bowl, combine the first six ingredients; set aside. Using 2-½-in. cookie cutters, cut stars and Christmas trees out of bread (two stars or trees from each slice). Spread half of the cutouts with crab mixture; top with remaining cutouts. Garnish with dill.

YIELD: 4 DOZEN.

Karen Gardiner, Eutaw, Alabama

To cool off during summer—or any season at all—
try the finger food that starts with a flavorful crab filling.
I regularly serve the spread at Christmas get-togethers.
It's a hit every time. For man-size sandwiches,
there's no need to use cookie cutters.

baked deli sandwich

1 loaf (1 pound) frozen bread dough, thawed

2 tablespoons butter, melted

¼ teaspoon garlic salt

¼ teaspoon dried basil

¼ teaspoon dried oregano

¼ teaspoon pizza seasoning

¼ pound sliced deli ham

6 thin slices mozzarella cheese

¼ pound sliced deli smoked turkey breast

6 thin slices cheddar cheese

Pizza sauce, warmed, optional

1 On a baking sheet coated with nonstick cooking spray, roll dough into a small rectangle. Let rest for 5-10 minutes.

2 In a small bowl, combine the butter and seasonings. Roll out dough into a 14-in. x 10-in. rectangle. Brush with half of the butter mixture. Layer ham, mozzarella cheese, turkey and cheddar cheese lengthwise over half of the dough to within ½ in. of edges. Fold dough over and pinch firmly to seal. Brush with remaining butter mixture.

3 Bake at 400° for 10-12 minutes or until golden brown. Cut into 1-in. slices. Serve immediately with pizza sauce if desired.

YIELD: 4-6 SERVINGS.

Sandra McKenzie, Braham, Minnesota

Frozen bread dough, easy assembly and quick baking time make this stuffed sandwich an appetizer I rely on often. This is one of my most-requested recipes. It's easy to double for a crowd or to experiment with different meats and cheeses.

garlic-cheese flat bread

1 tube (13.8 ounces) refrigerated pizza crust

¼ cup butter, melted

4 garlic cloves, minced

1 tablespoon minced fresh basil

1 cup (4 ounces) shredded cheddar cheese

½ cup grated Romano cheese

¼ cup grated Parmesan cheese

Press dough onto a greased 15-in. x 10-in. x 1-in. baking pan. In a small bowl, combine butter, garlic and basil; drizzle over dough. Sprinkle with the cheeses. Bake at 400° for 10-12 minutes or until crisp. Cut into squares. Serve warm.

YIELD: 12-15 SERVINGS.

Tom Hilliker, Lake Havasue City, Arizona

I use refrigerated pizza dough to create these savory squares with Italian flair. Serve them with a salad or soup, or try them as a snack with spaghetti sauce for dipping.

onion brie pizza

6 medium sweet onions, thinly sliced

¼ cup butter

1 package (16 ounces) hot roll mix

1¼ cups warm water (110° to 115°)

2 tablespoons olive oil

8 ounces Brie cheese, rind removed, and cut into small pieces

⅓ cup sliced almonds

1 In a large skillet, cook onions in butter over medium-low heat for 25 minutes or until golden brown, stirring occasionally.

2 Meanwhile, prepare hot roll mix according to package directions, using the warm water and oil. Place dough in a greased bowl, turning once to grease top. Cover and let stand for 5 minutes.

3 Roll out dough to a 14-in. circle; transfer to a greased 14-in. pizza pan. Top with onions, Brie and almonds. Bake at 400° for 18-20 minutes or until golden brown. Let stand for 10 minutes before cutting.

YIELD: 8 SERVINGS.

Cindy Bedell, West Layfayette, Indiana

Serve this unique pizza for a family supper or an elegant buffet.

beef 'n' cheese tortillas

½ cup garlic-herb cheese spread

4 flour tortillas (10 inches)

¾ pound thinly sliced cooked roast beef

20 to 25 whole spinach leaves

11 to 12 sweet banana peppers

Spread about 2 tablespoons cheese spread over each tortilla. Layer with roast beef and spinach. Remove seeds from peppers and slice into thin strips; arrange over spinach. Roll up each tortilla tightly; wrap in plastic wrap. Refrigerate until ready to serve.

YIELD: 4 SERVINGS.

Myra Innes, Auburn, Kansas

I like to take these sandwiches along on our many outings. They can be made in advance and don't get soggy. You'll appreciate the convenience, and your family and friends will love the great taste!

chicken french bread pizza

1 loaf (1 pound) French bread

½ cup butter, softened

½ cup shredded cheddar cheese

⅓ cup grated Parmesan cheese

1 garlic clove, minced

¼ teaspoon Italian seasoning

1 can (10 ounces) chunk white chicken, drained and flaked

1 cup (4 ounces) shredded part-skim mozzarella cheese

½ cup chopped sweet red pepper

½ cup chopped green onions

1 Cut bread in half lengthwise, then in half widthwise. Combine the butter, cheddar, Parmesan, garlic and Italian seasoning; spread over bread. Top with the remaining ingredients. Place on a baking sheet.

2 Bake at 350° for 10-12 minutes or until cheese is melted. Cut into smaller pieces if desired.

YIELD: 4 SERVINGS.

Laura Mahaffey, Annapolis, Maryland
This pizza makes a hearty snack for TV game
night or as an after-school treat.

ham and cheese bread

1 package (16 ounces) frozen chopped broccoli

2 loaves (1 pound *each*) frozen bread dough, thawed

3 cups (12 ounces) shredded cheese (cheddar, Swiss *and/or* Monterey Jack)

2 cups finely chopped fully cooked ham

2 tablespoons butter, melted

1 teaspoon poppy seeds

1 Cook broccoli according to package directions. Drain and cool.

2 Roll each loaf of dough into a 15-in. x 10-in. rectangle. Place one in a greased 15-in. x 10-in. x 1-in. baking pan. Sprinkle with the broccoli, cheese and ham to within ½ in. of edges. Place second rectangle on top, sealing edges.

3 Brush the top with butter; sprinkle with poppy seeds. Bake at 350° for 35-40 minutes or until golden brown. Serve warm.

YIELD: 10-12 SERVINGS.

Marian Christensen, Sumner, Michigan

Ham and cheese baked inside bread dough makes a hearty snack. The broccoli adds a bit of color.

italian cheese loaf

1 loaf (1 pound) French bread

2 cups diced fresh tomatoes

1 cup (4 ounces) shredded part-skim mozzarella cheese

1 cup (4 ounces) shredded cheddar cheese

1 medium onion, finely chopped

¼ cup grated Romano cheese

¼ cup chopped ripe olives

¼ cup Italian salad dressing

1 teaspoon chopped fresh basil

1 teaspoon chopped fresh oregano

1 Cut top half off loaf of bread; set aside. Carefully hollow out bottom of loaf, leaving a ½-in. shell (discard removed bread or save for another use).

2 In a bowl, combine the remaining ingredients. Spoon into bread shell; replace top. Wrap in foil. Bake at 350° for 25 minutes or until cheese is melted. Slice and serve warm.

YIELD: 12 SERVINGS.

Mary Ann Marino, West Pittsburg, Pennsylvania

Here's a deliciously different sandwich. It's yummy warm from the oven or off the grill at a cookout. The cheesy filling is complemented by a mix of garden-fresh tomatoes and herbs and crusty bread.

chicken quesadillas

4 cups all-purpose flour

1½ teaspoons salt

½ teaspoon baking powder

1 cup shortening

1¼ cups warm water

1 cup *each* shredded cheddar, part-skim mozzarella and pepper Jack cheese

2 cups diced cooked chicken

1 cup sliced green onions

1 cup sliced ripe olives

1 can (4 ounces) chopped green chilies, drained

Salsa and sour cream

1 In a bowl, combine the flour, salt and baking powder. Cut in shortening until crumbly. Add enough warm water, stirring until mixture forms a ball. Let stand for 10 minutes. Divide into 28 portions.

2 On a lightly floured surface, roll each portion into a 7-in. circle. Cook on a lightly greased griddle for 1½ to 2 minutes on each side, breaking any bubbles with a toothpick if necessary. Keep warm.

3 In a bowl, combine the cheeses. For each quesadilla, place a tortilla on the griddle; sprinkle with about 2 tablespoons cheese mixture, 2 tablespoons chicken, 1 tablespoon onions, 1 tablespoon olives and 1 teaspoon chilies. Top with 1 tablespoon cheese mixture and another tortilla. Cook for 30-60 seconds; turn and cook 30 seconds longer or until cheese is melted. Cut into wedges. Serve with the salsa and sour cream.

YIELD: 14 QUESADILLAS.

Linda Miller, Klamath Falls, Oregon
Tender homemade tortillas make this savory snack, filled with chicken and melted cheese, extra-special.

ham buns

½ cup butter, softened

1 small onion, grated

1 tablespoon poppy seeds

2 teaspoons Worcestershire sauce

2 teaspoons prepared mustard

1¼ cups finely chopped fully cooked ham (about 8 ounces)

1 cup (4 ounces) shredded Swiss cheese

6 to 8 hamburger buns, split *or* 16 to 20 mini buns

1 In a bowl, combine the butter, onion, poppy seeds, Worcestershire sauce and mustard. Add ham and cheese; mix well. Divide evenly among buns.

2 Place in a shallow baking pan and cover with foil. Bake at 350° for 15 to 20 minutes or until hot.

YIELD: 6-8 MAIN DISH OR 16-20 APPETIZER SERVINGS.

Esther Shank, Harrisonburg, Virginia

These tasty sandwiches are a great way to use leftover ham. Friends with whom I've shared the recipe tell me that Ham Buns disappear fast at potlucks or parties. Use mini-buns and make ahead for an easy meal or snack.

mozzarella pepperoni bread

1 loaf (1 pound) French bread

3 tablespoons butter, melted

3 ounces sliced turkey pepperoni

1½ cups (6 ounces) shredded part-skim mozzarella cheese

3 tablespoons minced fresh parsley

1 Cut loaf of bread in half widthwise; cut into 1-in. slices, leaving slices attached at bottom. Brush butter on both sides of each slice. Arrange pepperoni between slices; sprinkle with cheese and parsley.

2 Place on an ungreased baking sheet. Bake at 350° for 12-15 minutes or until cheese is melted.

YIELD: 24 SLICES.

Terri Toti, San Antonio, Texas

My family enjoys this tempting bread as an appetizer when we have company, and as a quick meal on hectic evenings.

deli vegetable roll-ups

½ cup garden vegetable cream
   cheese spread

4 flour tortillas (10 inches)

1 medium tomato, seeded and diced

2 sweet banana peppers, seeded
   and julienned

1 cup sliced ripe olives

4 slices Colby cheese

4 slices part-skim mozzarella cheese

8 thick dill pickle slices

¼ cup ranch salad dressing

4 lettuce leaves

4 thinly sliced deli turkey

4 thin slices salami

Additional ranch salad dressing, optional

Spread about 2 tablespoons of cream cheese spread over each tortilla. Layer with tomato, peppers, olives, cheeses and pickle slices. Drizzle with salad dressing. Top with the lettuce, turkey and salami. Roll up tightly; wrap in plastic wrap. Refrigerate until ready to serve. Serve with additional dressing if desired.

YIELD: 4 SERVINGS.

Nancy Divelbiss, Leo, Indiana

I make these loaded tortilla sandwiches for my husband and son for lunch or for a snack. My son thought I could peddle them on a street corner—and be sold out in an hour!

artichoke veggie pizza

1 tube (13.8 ounces) refrigerated pizza crust

1 package (8 ounces) cream cheese, softened

½ cup sun-dried tomato spread

1 can (14 ounces) water-packed artichoke hearts, rinsed, drained and finely chopped

½ cup chopped sweet onion

1 can (4¼ ounces) chopped ripe olives, drained

¾ cup sliced carrots

¾ cup chopped green pepper

1½ cups fresh broccoli florets, chopped

1 cup (4 ounces) shredded Italian cheese blend

1 Press pizza dough into a greased 15-in. x 10-in. x 1-in. baking pan. Prick dough thoroughly with a fork. Bake at 400° for 13-15 minutes or until golden brown. Cool.

2 In a small mixing bowl, beat cream cheese and tomato spread until blended. Stir in the artichokes. Spread over crust. Sprinkle with the onion, olives, carrots, green pepper, broccoli and cheese; press down lightly. Refrigerate for 1 hour. Cut into squares. Refrigerate leftovers.

YIELD: 3 DOZEN.

Taste of Home Test Kitchen

A sun-dried tomato spread is used as the base for this vegetable-laden appetizer.

double sausage pizza

1 package (16 ounces) hot roll mix

2 tablespoons garlic powder

2 tablespoons dried oregano

2 tablespoons Italian seasoning

1¼ cups warm water (120° to 130°)

2 tablespoons vegetable oil

1 can (15 ounces) pizza sauce

½ cup grated Parmesan cheese

1 pound bulk pork sausage, cooked and crumbled

½ pound sliced fresh mushrooms

1 package (8 ounces) sliced pepperoni

4 cups (28 ounces) shredded part-skim mozzarella cheese

1 In a large bowl, combine the hot roll mix, contents of yeast packet, garlic powder, oregano and Italian seasoning. Stir in water and oil until dough pulls away from sides of bowl. Turn dough onto a lightly floured surface. Shape into a ball. Knead for 5 minutes or until smooth. Cover and let stand for 5 minutes.

2 Divide dough in half. With greased hands, press dough onto two greased 12-in. pizza pans. Prick dough thoroughly with a fork. Spread crusts with pizza sauce. Top with the Parmesan cheese, sausage, mushrooms, pepperoni and mozzarella cheese. Bake at 425° for 18-20 minutes or until cheese is melted.

YIELD: 2 PIZZAS (8-10 SLICES EACH).

Emalee Satoski, Union Mills, Indiana

This recipe has been in the family since I was a kid. It was a Sunday night ritual then, and remains one today in my home. A dressed-up hot roll mix gives us enough dough for two flavorful crusts, so there is plenty of sausage-pepperoni pizza to serve company.

kielbasa bundles

½ pound fully cooked kielbasa *or* Polish sausage, chopped

1 small onion, chopped

¼ cup chopped green pepper

1 garlic clove, minced

1 tablespoon butter

⅓ cup barbecue sauce

2 tubes (8 ounces *each*) refrigerated crescent rolls

4 slices process American cheese, halved

1 egg white

1 tablespoon water

Sesame seeds

1 In a large skillet, cook sausage for 5-8 minutes; drain. Add the onion, green pepper, garlic and butter; cook until vegetables are tender. Stir in barbecue sauce; heat through.

2 Unroll crescent roll dough and separate into eight rectangles; seal perforations. Place a cheese slice on half of each rectangle; top with 2 tablespoons sausage mixture. Fold dough over filling and pinch edges to seal; fold seam under. Beat egg white and water; brush over dough. Sprinkle with sesame seeds.

3 Place bundles seam side down on greased baking sheets. Bake at 350° for 15-18 minutes or until golden brown.

YIELD: 8 SERVINGS.

Robin Touchey, San Angelo, Texas
My family really enjoys these flavorful sandwiches.

herbed onion focaccia

Melanie Eddy, Manhattan, Kansas

This recipe makes three savory flat breads, but don't be surprised to see them all disappear from the table!

1 tablespoon active dry yeast

1 teaspoon sugar

1½ cups warm water (110° to 115°), *divided*

6 tablespoons olive oil, *divided*

2 teaspoons salt

4 to 4½ cups all-purpose flour

3 tablespoons finely chopped green onions

1½ teaspoons minced fresh rosemary *or* ½ teaspoon dried rosemary, crushed

1½ teaspoons small fresh sage leaves *or* ½ teaspoon rubbed sage

1½ teaspoons minced fresh oregano plus ½ teaspoon dried oregano

Seasoned olive oil *or* additional olive oil, optional

1 In a large mixing bowl, dissolve yeast and sugar in ½ cup warm water; let stand for 5 minutes. Add 4 tablespoons oil, salt, 2 cups flour and remaining water. Beat until smooth. Stir enough remaining flour to form a soft dough.

2 Turn onto a floured surface; knead until smooth and elastic, about 6-8 minutes. Place in a greased bowl, turning once to grease top. Cover and let rise in a warm place until doubled, about 1 hour.

3 Punch dough down. Divide into three portions. Cover and let rest for 10 minutes. Shape each portion into an 8-in. circle; place on greased baking sheets. Cover and let rise until doubled, about 30 minutes.

4 Using the end of a wooden spoon handle, make several ¼-in. indentations in each loaf. Brush with remaining oil. Sprinkle with green onions, rosemary, sage and oregano. Bake at 400° for 20-25 minutes or until golden brown. Remove to wire racks. Serve with olive oil for dipping if desired.

YIELD: 3 LOAVES.

cranberry camembert pizza

1 tube (13.8 ounces) refrigerated pizza crust

8 ounces Camembert *or* Brie cheese, rind removed and cut into ½-inch cubes

¾ cup whole-berry cranberry sauce

½ cup chopped pecans

1 Unroll crust onto a lightly greased 12-in. pizza pan; flatten dough and build up edges slightly. Bake at 425° for 10-12 minutes or until light golden brown.

2 Sprinkle cheese over crust. Spoon cranberry sauce evenly over crust; sprinkle with pecans. Bake 8-10 minutes longer or until the cheese is melted and crust is golden brown. Cool for 5 minutes before cutting.

YIELD: 12-14 SLICES.

Heidi Mellon, Waukesha, Wisconsin

After I'd tasted this quick, yummy pizza at a party, I just knew I had to have the recipe. I've been serving it in my household for years, and it always disappears in minutes.

guacamole turkey subs

1 package (3 ounces) cream cheese, softened

1/3 cup prepared guacamole

1/4 cup picante sauce

3 submarine sandwich buns (about 8 inches), split

1 1/2 cups shredded lettuce

1 medium tomato, thinly sliced

9 slices smoked deli turkey

9 bacon strips, cooked and drained

In a bowl, combine the cream cheese, guacamole and picante sauce; spread over cut side of buns. On bun bottoms, layer half of the lettuce, all of the tomato, turkey and bacon, then remaining lettuce. Replace tops. Cut sandwiches in half; wrap in plastic wrap. Refrigerate until serving.

YIELD: 6 SERVINGS.

Marci McDonald, Amarillo, Texas

This may sound like a strange combination, but it is without a doubt the best sandwich you'll ever eat!

salsa strips

1 tube (8 ounces) refrigerated crescent rolls

2 tablespoons Dijon mustard

3/4 cup salsa

1 cup (4 ounces) shredded part-skim mozzarella cheese

Minced fresh cilantro

1 Unroll crescent roll dough and separate into four rectangles. Place on greased baking sheets. Spread mustard and salsa on each rectangle.

2 Bake at 350° for 10 minutes. Sprinkle with cheese; bake 8-10 minutes longer or until golden brown. Cool for 10 minutes. Cut each into four strips; sprinkle with cilantro.

YIELD: 16 APPETIZERS.

Joann Woloszyn, Fredonia, New York

Refrigerated crescent rolls make these crisp Southwestern appetizers a breeze to prepare. Choose mild, medium or hot salsa to suit your taste.

wings & more

120

132

Watch your guests flock to trays of party favorites, featuring wings, meatballs, sausages and shrimp. Be sure to have plenty of napkins on hand when you serve these saucy delights, including Orange-Glazed Chicken Wings (p. 129), Glazed Meatballs (p. 121), Stuffed Butterfly Shrimp (p. 120) or Chicken Bacon Bites (p. 132).

Use a chafing dish or slow cooker to keep these tempting tidbits warm. To make last-minute preparations simple, choose recipes you can whip up the day before and just reheat when your guests arrive.

cranberry meatballs and sausage

1 egg, beaten

1 small onion, finely chopped

¾ cup dry bread crumbs

1 tablespoon dried parsley flakes

1 tablespoon Worcestershire sauce

¼ teaspoon salt

1 pound bulk pork sausage

1 can (16 ounces) jellied cranberry
sauce

3 tablespoons cider vinegar

2 tablespoons brown sugar

1 tablespoon prepared mustard

1 package (1 pound) miniature
smoked sausage links

1 In a large bowl, combine the first six ingredients. Crumble bulk sausage over the mixture and mix well. Shape into 1-in. balls. In a large skillet, cook meatballs over medium heat until browned; drain.

2 In a large saucepan, combine the cranberry sauce, vinegar, brown sugar and mustard. Cook and stir over medium heat until cranberry sauce is melted. Add the meatballs and sausage links. Bring to a boil. Reduce heat; simmer, uncovered, for 10-15 minutes or until meatballs are no longer pink and sauce is slightly thickened.

YIELD: 14-16 SERVINGS.

Marybell Lintott, Vernon, British Columbia

Years ago, I found a version of this recipe in a cookbook. At first taste, my family judged it a keeper. The tangy, saucy meatballs are requested by our friends whenever I host card night. We also take the yummy dish on camping trips.

bandito chicken wings

12 whole chicken wings (about 2 pounds)

½ teaspoon salt

⅛ teaspoon pepper

½ cup butter, *divided*

2 tablespoons vegetable oil

½ cup taco sauce

¼ cup barbecue sauce

¼ cup French salad dressing

1 teaspoon Worcestershire sauce

⅛ teaspoon hot pepper sauce

1 Cut chicken wings into three sections; discard wing tips. Sprinkle with salt and pepper. In a skillet, melt 2 tablespoons butter with oil over medium. Fry chicken until brown, about 6-8 minutes on each side. Place in a greased 13-in. x 9-in. x 2-in. baking dish.

2 In a saucepan, combine the taco sauce, barbecue sauce, French dressing, Worcestershire sauce, hot pepper sauce and the remaining butter; cook and stir over medium heat until butter is melted and sauce is blended. Pour ½ cup over the chicken wings.

3 Bake, uncovered, at 325° for 15-20 minutes or until chicken juices run clear. Serve with the remaining sauce.

YIELD: 8-10 SERVINGS.

EDITOR'S NOTE: This recipe was prepared with the first and second sections of the chicken wings.

Gloria Jarrett, Loveland, Ohio
These fantastic wings make a mouth-watering, hot and spicy appetizer.

chicken satay

Sue Gronholz, Beaver Dam, Wisconsin

These golden skewered chicken snacks are marinated and grilled, then served with a zesty Thai-style peanut butter sauce.

2 pounds boneless skinless chicken breasts

1/2 cup milk

6 garlic cloves, minced

1 tablespoon brown sugar

1 tablespoon *each* ground coriander, ground turmeric and ground cumin

1 teaspoon salt

1 teaspoon white pepper

1/8 teaspoon coconut extract

PEANUT BUTTER SAUCE:

1/3 cup peanut butter

1/3 cup milk

2 green onions, chopped

1 small jalapeno pepper, seeded and finely chopped

2 to 3 tablespoons lime juice

2 tablespoons soy sauce

1 garlic clove, minced

1 teaspoon sugar

1 teaspoon minced fresh cilantro

1 teaspoon minced fresh gingerroot

1/8 teaspoon coconut extract

1 Flatten chicken to 1/4-in. thickness; cut lengthwise into 1-in.-wide strips. In a large resealable plastic bag, combine the milk, garlic, brown sugar, seasonings and extract. Add chicken; seal bag and turn to coat. Refrigerate for 8 hours or overnight.

2 In a bowl, whisk the sauce ingredients until blended. Cover and refrigerate until serving. Drain and discard marinade from chicken. Thread two chicken strips onto each metal or soaked wooden skewer.

3 Grill, uncovered, over medium-hot heat for 2-3 minutes on each side or until chicken juices run clear. Serve with peanut butter sauce.

YIELD: 8 SERVINGS (1 CUP SAUCE).

EDITOR'S NOTE: When cutting or seeding hot peppers, use rubber or plastic gloves to protect your hands. Avoid touching your face.

enchilada meatballs

2 cups crumbled corn bread

1 can (10 ounces) enchilada sauce, *divided*

1/2 teaspoon salt

1 1/2 pounds ground beef

1 can (8 ounces) tomato sauce

1/2 cup shredded Mexican cheese blend

1 In a large bowl, combine the corn bread, 1/2 cup enchilada sauce and salt. Crumble beef over mixture; mix well. Shape into 1-in. balls.

2 Place in a greased 15-in. x 10-in. x 1-in. baking pan. Bake, uncovered, at 350° for 18-22 minutes or until meat is no longer pink.

3 Meanwhile, in a small saucepan, heat tomato sauce and remaining enchilada sauce. Drain meatballs; place in a serving dish. Top with sauce and sprinkle with cheese. Serve with toothpicks.

YIELD: ABOUT 4 1/2 DOZEN.

Marcia Harris, Stevensville, Michigan
Before I retired, these tasty little treats were popular during snack time at work. They're a good way to use up leftover corn bread.

coconut shrimp

1¼ cups all-purpose flour

¼ teaspoon seafood seasoning

1 egg, beaten

¾ cup pineapple juice

1 package (14 ounces) flaked coconut

1 pound large shrimp, peeled and deveined

Oil for deep-fat frying

Sweet-and-sour sauce, plum sauce or Dijon mustard, optional

1 In a bowl, combine the flour, seasoning, egg and pineapple juice until smooth. Place coconut in a shallow bowl. Dip shrimp into batter, then coat with coconut.

2 In an electric skillet or deep-fat fryer, heat oil to 375°. Fry shrimp, a few at a time, for 1½ minutes or until golden brown, turning occasionally. Drain on paper towels. Serve with dipping sauce or mustard if desired.

YIELD: ABOUT 1½ DOZEN.

Tacy Holliday, Germantown, Maryland
Guests are always impressed when I present these restaurant-quality shrimp. A selection of sauces served alongside adds the perfect touch.

stuffed butterflied shrimp

24 uncooked unpeeled large shrimp

1 cup Italian salad dressing

1½ cups seasoned bread crumbs

1 can (6½ ounces) chopped clams, drained and minced

6 tablespoons butter, melted

1½ teaspoons minced fresh parsley

1 Peel shrimp, leaving tail section on. Make a deep cut along the top of each shrimp (do not cut all the way through); remove the vein. Place shrimp in a shallow dish; add salad dressing. Set aside for 20 minutes.

2 Meanwhile, in a large bowl, combine the bread crumbs, clams, butter and parsley. Drain and discard salad dressing. Arrange shrimp in a greased 13-in. x 9-in. x 2-in. baking dish. Open shrimp and press flat; fill each with 1 tablespoon of crumb mixture. Bake, uncovered, at 350° for 20-25 minutes or until shrimp turn pink.

YIELD: 2 DOZEN.

Joan Elliott, Deep River, Connecticut

These flavorful, baked shrimp can be an appetizer or entree. I've handed out this recipe to many friends and family members.

glazed meatballs

2 eggs

⅔ cup milk

1¼ cups soft bread crumbs

1 tablespoon prepared horseradish

1½ pounds ground beef

1 cup water

½ cup chili sauce

½ cup ketchup

¼ cup maple syrup

¼ cup soy sauce

1½ teaspoons ground allspice

½ teaspoon ground mustard

1 In a bowl, beat eggs and milk. Stir in bread crumbs and horseradish. Crumble beef over mixture and mix well. Shape into 1½-in. balls.

2 Place in a lightly greased 15-in x 10-in. x 1-in. baking pan. Bake at 375° for 15-20 minutes or until meat is no longer pink.

3 In a large saucepan, combine the remaining ingredients. Bring to a boil; add the meatballs. Reduce heat; cover and simmer for 15 minutes or until heated through, stirring occasionally.

YIELD: ABOUT 3½ DOZEN.

Nancy Horsburgh, Everett, Ontario

Allspice adds a bit of a twist to the barbecue-style sauce used in this recipe.

garlic-cheese chicken wings

2 large whole garlic bulbs

1 tablespoon plus ½ cup olive oil, *divided*

½ cup butter, melted

1 teaspoon hot pepper sauce

1½ cups seasoned bread crumbs

¾ cup grated Parmesan cheese

¾ cup grated Romano cheese

½ teaspoon pepper

15 whole chicken wings (about 3 pounds)

1 Remove papery outer skin from garlic (do not peel or separate cloves). Cut top off garlic bulbs. Brush with 1 tablespoon oil. Wrap each bulb in heavy-duty foil. Bake at 425° for 30-35 minutes or until softened. Cool for 10-15 minutes.

2 Squeeze the softened garlic into a blender or food processor. Add butter, hot pepper sauce and remaining oil; cover and process until smooth. Pour into a shallow bowl. In another shallow bowl, combine the bread crumbs, cheeses and pepper.

3 Cut chicken wings into three sections; discard wing tip section. Dip chicken wings into the garlic mixture, then coat with crumb mixture. Place on a greased rack in a 15-in. x 10-in. x 1-in. baking pan; drizzle with any remaining garlic mixture. Bake, uncovered, at 350° for 50-55 minutes or until chicken juices run clear.

YIELD: 2½ DOZEN.

EDITOR'S NOTE: 3 pounds of uncooked chicken wing sections (wingettes) may be substituted for the whole chicken wings. Omit the third step.

Donna Pierce, Lady Lake, Florida

I developed this recipe several years ago using chicken breasts, then decided to try it on wings as an appetizer, and it was a hit! If you like garlic, you're sure to enjoy these tender, zesty bites.

flavorful sausage balls

1 pound bulk pork sausage

1 egg, beaten

1/2 cup dry bread crumbs

3/4 cup ketchup

1/4 cup packed brown sugar

2 tablespoons white vinegar

2 tablespoons soy sauce

1 In a bowl, combine sausage and egg. Sprinkle with bread crumbs; mix well. Shape into 1-in. balls.

2 In a skillet, brown meatballs; drain. Combine remaining ingredients; pour over meatballs. Simmer for 10 minutes or until meat is no longer pink.

YIELD: 2 1/2 DOZEN.

Olive Lamb, Cushing, Oklahoma

I whip up a batch of these meatballs in a matter of minutes. They're a great treat on busy days when you need something fast that's full of flavor.

ginger meatballs

1 egg

1/2 cup finely crushed gingersnaps (about 11 cookies)

1 teaspoon salt

1 1/2 pounds ground beef

1 cup ketchup

1/4 cup packed brown sugar

2 tablespoons Dijon mustard

1/2 teaspoon ground ginger

1 In a large bowl, combine the egg, cookie crumbs and salt. Crumble beef over mixture and mix well. Shape into 1-in. balls. Place 1 in. apart in ungreased 15-in. x 10-in. x 1-in. baking pans. Bake, uncovered, at 350° for 15-20 minutes or until no longer pink; drain.

2 In a large skillet, combine ketchup, brown sugar, mustard and ginger. Add meatballs. Simmer, uncovered, for 15-20 minutes or until heated through, gently stirring several times.

YIELD: ABOUT 3 1/2 DOZEN.

Sybil Leson, Houston, Texas

These sweet and tangy meatballs have caused many guests to ask, "What is that delicious flavor?" For a crowd, double the recipe and keep them warm in a slow cooker.

sweet-sour sausage bites

½ pound smoked sausage, cut into ½-inch slices

1 can (20 ounces) pineapple chunks

4 teaspoons cornstarch

½ teaspoon salt

½ cup maple syrup

⅓ cup water

⅓ cup white vinegar

1 large green pepper, cut into ¾-inch pieces

½ cup maraschino cherries

1 In a large skillet, saute the sausage for 3-5 minutes or until lightly browned. Drain on paper towels; set aside. Drain pineapple, reserving juice; set the pineapple aside.

2 In a large skillet, combine the cornstarch, salt and reserved pineapple juice until smooth. Stir in the syrup, water and vinegar. Bring to a boil; cook and stir for 2-3 minutes or until thickened. Add the sausage, green pepper, cherries and pineapple. Simmer, uncovered, for 5 minutes or until peppers are crisp-tender. Transfer to a shallow serving dish. Serve with toothpicks.

YIELD: 4 CUPS.

Maretta Bullock, McNeil, Arkansas

As a pastor's wife, I frequently entertain church groups in my home, so I'm always looking for new recipes. These quick and easy appetizers are not only delicious, they're colorful, too. I've made them many times.

nuggets with chili sauce

1 cup chicken broth

2 cans (4 ounces *each*) chopped green chilies

2 medium onions, diced

3 tablespoons butter

1 tablespoon chili powder

2 teaspoons ground cumin

2 garlic cloves, minced

¼ cup packed brown sugar

¼ cup orange juice

¼ cup ketchup

2 tablespoons lemon juice

CHICKEN NUGGETS:

½ cup cornmeal

1 tablespoon chili powder

2 teaspoons ground cumin

¼ teaspoon salt

1½ pounds boneless skinless chicken breasts, cut into 1-inch cubes

3 tablespoons vegetable oil

1 In blender or food processor, combine broth and chilies; cover and process until pureed. Set aside. In a large skillet, saute onions in butter until tender. Stir in the chili powder, cumin, garlic and pureed mixture. Bring to a boil. Reduce heat to low; simmer, uncovered, for 20 minutes, stirring occasionally.

2 Add the brown sugar, orange juice, ketchup and lemon juice. Cook and stir over low heat for 15 minutes or until thickened; keep warm.

3 For nuggets, combine the cornmeal, chili powder, cumin and salt in a large resealable plastic bag. Add chicken pieces, a few at a time, to bag; shake to coat. Heat oil in skillet; cook chicken for 6-8 minutes or until juices run clear, turning frequently. Serve with sauce.

YIELD: 4 SERVINGS.

Diane Hixon, Niceville, Florida

These crisp golden bites of chicken taste better than the fast-food versions. The chili sauce really sets them apart from any others.

honey-garlic glazed meatballs

2 eggs

¾ cup milk

1 cup dry bread crumbs

½ cup finely chopped onion

2 teaspoons salt

2 pounds ground beef

4 garlic cloves, minced

1 tablespoon butter

¾ cup ketchup

½ cup honey

3 tablespoons soy sauce

1 In a large bowl, combine eggs and milk. Add the bread crumbs, onion and salt. Crumble beef over mixture and mix well. Shape into 1-in. balls. Place in two greased 15-in. x 10-in. x 1-in. baking pans. Bake, uncovered, at 400° for 12-15 minutes or until meat is no longer pink.

2 Meanwhile, in a large saucepan, saute garlic in butter until tender. Stir in the ketchup, honey and soy sauce. Bring to a boil. Reduce heat; cover and simmer for 5 minutes. Drain meatballs; add to sauce. Carefully stir to evenly coat. Cook for 5-10 minutes.

YIELD: 5½ DOZEN.

Marion Foster, Kirkton, Ontario

My husband and I raise cattle on our farm here in southwestern Ontario, so it's no surprise that we're fond of these juicy meatballs. I know your family will like them, too.

coconut chicken bites

2 cups flaked coconut

1 egg

2 tablespoons milk

¾ pound boneless skinless chicken breasts, cut into ¾-inch pieces

½ cup all-purpose flour

Oil for deep-fat frying

1 teaspoon celery salt

½ teaspoon garlic powder

½ teaspoon ground cumin

1 In a blender or food processor, process coconut until finely chopped. Transfer to a bowl and set aside. In another bowl, combine egg and milk. Toss chicken with flour; dip in egg mixture, then in coconut. Place in a single layer on a baking sheet. Refrigerate for 30 minutes.

2 In an electric skillet or deep-fat fryer, heat 2 in. of oil to 375°. Fry chicken, a few pieces at time, for 1½ minutes on each side or until golden brown. Drain on paper towels; place in a bowl. Sprinkle with celery salt, garlic powder and cumin; toss to coat. Serve warm.

YIELD: 3 DOZEN.

Linda Schwarz, Bertrand, Nebraska
These tender nuggets are great for nibbling, thanks to the coconut and seasonings. I've served these bites several times at parties, and everyone enjoyed them.

chicken meatball appetizers

2½ cups minced cooked chicken breast

3 tablespoons finely chopped onion

3 tablespoons finely chopped celery

2 tablespoons finely chopped carrot

2 tablespoons dry bread crumbs

1 egg white

½ teaspoon poultry seasoning

Pinch pepper

In a bowl, combine all ingredients; mix well. Shape into ¾-in. balls; place on a baking sheet that has been coated with nonstick cooking spray. Bake at 400° for 8-10 minutes or until lightly browned.

YIELD: ABOUT 2½ DOZEN.

Norma Snider, Chambersburg, Pennsylvania
Here's a crowd-pleasing change of pace on the appetizer tray. Try these chicken meatballs plain or dipped in mustard.

honey-mustard turkey meatballs

1 egg, lightly beaten

¾ cup crushed butter-flavored crackers

½ cup shredded part-skim mozzarella cheese

¼ cup chopped onion

½ teaspoon ground ginger

6 tablespoons Dijon mustard, *divided*

1 pound ground turkey

1 tablespoon cornstarch

¼ teaspoon onion powder

1¼ cups unsweetened pineapple juice

¼ cup chopped green pepper

2 tablespoons honey

1 In a bowl, combine the egg, cracker crumbs, cheese, onion, ginger and 3 tablespoons mustard. Crumble turkey over mixture and mix well. Shape into 30 (1-in.) balls. Place in a greased 13-in. x 9-in x. 2-in. baking dish. Bake, uncovered, at 350° for 20-25 minutes or until juices run clear.

2 In a saucepan, combine the cornstarch and onion powder. Stir in the pineapple juice until smooth. Add the pepper and honey. Bring to a boil; cook and stir 2 minutes or until thickened. Reduce heat; stir in remaining mustard until smooth.

3 Brush meatballs with about ¼ cup sauce and bake 10 minutes longer. Serve remaining sauce as a dip for meatballs.

YIELD: 2½ DOZEN.

Bonnie Durkin, Nescopeck, Pennsylvania

I serve this appetizer often during the holidays. It's nice to have a turkey meatball that doesn't taste like you should have used beef. These tangy meatballs can be prepared ahead and frozen, so even drop-in guests can be treated to a hot snack.

orange-glazed chicken wings

15 whole chicken wings (about 3 pounds)

1½ cups soy sauce

1 cup orange juice

1 teaspoon garlic powder

1 Cut chicken wings into three sections; discard wing tips. In a large resealable plastic bag, combine the soy sauce, orange juice and garlic powder; add wings. Seal bag and turn to coat; refrigerate overnight.

2 Drain and discard marinade. Place chicken wings in a greased foil-lined 15-in. x 10-in. x 1-in. baking pan. Bake at 350° for 1 hour or until juices run clear and glaze is set, turning twice.

YIELD: 2½ DOZEN.

EDITOR'S NOTE: 3 pounds of uncooked chicken wingettes may be substituted for the whole chicken wings. Omit the first step.

Holly Mann, Amherst, New Hampshire

I normally don't care for wings, but after I tried this recipe that was shared by a co-worker, it changed my mind about these lovely glazed wings.

sesame chicken bites

½ cup dry bread crumbs

¼ cup sesame seeds

2 teaspoons minced fresh parsley

½ cup mayonnaise

1 teaspoon onion powder

1 teaspoon ground mustard

¼ teaspoon pepper

1 pound boneless skinless chicken breasts, cut into 1-inch cubes

2 to 4 tablespoons vegetable oil

HONEY-MUSTARD SAUCE:

¾ cup mayonnaise

4½ teaspoons honey

1½ teaspoons Dijon mustard

1 In a large resealable plastic bag, combine the bread crumbs, sesame seeds and parsley; set aside. In a small bowl, combine the mayonnaise, onion powder, mustard and pepper. Coat chicken in mayonnaise mixture, then add to crumb mixture, a few pieces at a time; shake to coat.

2 In a large skillet, cook chicken in oil in batches until juices run clear, adding additional oil as needed. In a small bowl, combine the sauce ingredients. Serve with the chicken.

YIELD: 8-10 SERVINGS.

Kathy Green, Layton, New Jersey

So tender and tasty, these chicken appetizers are enhanced by a honey-mustard dipping sauce. I used to spend several days creating hors d'oeuvres for our holiday open house, and these bites were among the favorites.

sweet-and-sour sausages

2 packages (16 ounces *each*) miniature smoked sausages

2 tablespoons butter

1 can (15¼ ounces) sliced peaches, drained and halved

1 cup chili sauce

¾ cup sugar

½ cup ketchup

1 teaspoon dried minced onion

1 teaspoon curry powder

1 In a large skillet, brown sausages in butter. In a large bowl, combine the remaining ingredients; stir in the sausages. Transfer to a greased 2-qt. baking dish.

2 Bake, uncovered, at 350° for 30 minutes. Stir; bake 15 minutes longer or until bubbly.

YIELD: 18 SERVINGS.

Dorothy Anderson, Langley, British Columbia

A perfect buffet appetizer, these zesty links also make a great main course. I've prepared them so often that I can recite the recipe from memory.

skewered shrimp

3 tablespoons soy sauce

2 tablespoons lemon juice

1 tablespoon chili sauce

1 tablespoon minced fresh gingerroot

1 pound uncooked medium shrimp, peeled and deveined

1 In a bowl, combine the soy sauce, lemon juice, chili sauce and ginger; mix well. Pour half into a large resealable plastic bag; add the shrimp. Seal bag and turn to coat; refrigerate for 2 hours. Cover and refrigerate remaining marinade.

2 Drain and discard marinade from shrimp. Thread onto metal or soaked wooden skewers. Grill, uncovered, over medium heat for 6-8 minutes or until shrimp turn pink, turning once. Serve with reserved marinade.

YIELD: 4 SERVINGS.

Joan Morris, Lillian, Alabama

A ginger mixture is used as both a marinade and a sauce for these barbecued shrimp. Serve them with toothpicks as an appetizer or stir into pasta for an entree.

chicken bacon bites

Betty Pierson, Wellington, Florida

Ginger and orange marmalade give these rumaki-style snacks wonderful flavor. I marinate the wrapped chicken earlier in the day and broil them when guests arrive.

12 bacon strips, halved

10 ounces boneless skinless chicken breasts, cut into 24 cubes

 1 can (8 ounces) sliced water chestnuts, drained

½ cup orange marmalade

¼ cup soy sauce

 2 garlic cloves, minced

 1 teaspoon grated fresh gingerroot

1 Place bacon on a broiler rack. Broil 4 in. from the heat for 1-2 minutes on each side or until partially cooked; cool.

2 Wrap a piece of bacon around a chicken cube and water chestnut slice; secure with a toothpick. In a resealable plastic bag, combine the marmalade, soy sauce, garlic and ginger. Add wrapped chicken; carefully turn to coat. Seal and refrigerate for 2 hours.

3 Drain and discard marinade. Broil chicken for 3-4 minutes on each side or until juices run clear and bacon is crisp. Serve warm.

YIELD: 2 DOZEN.

shrimp on rosemary skewers

8 fresh rosemary sprigs, about 6 inches long

$\frac{1}{2}$ cup orange marmalade

$\frac{1}{2}$ cup flaked coconut, chopped

$\frac{1}{4}$ teaspoon crushed red pepper flakes

$\frac{1}{4}$ teaspoon minced fresh rosemary

$1\frac{1}{2}$ pounds uncooked large shrimp, peeled and deveined

1 Soak rosemary sprigs in water for 30 minutes. In a small bowl, combine the marmalade, coconut, pepper flakes and minced rosemary; set aside $\frac{1}{4}$ cup for serving.

2 Coat grill rack with nonstick cooking spray before starting the grill. Thread shrimp onto rosemary sprigs. Grill for 4 minutes. Turn; baste with some of the remaining marmalade mixture. Grill 3-4 minutes longer or until shrimp turn pink; baste again. Serve with reserved marmalade mixture.

YIELD: 8 SERVINGS.

Amber Joy Newport, Hampton, Virginia

Fresh springs of rosemary are the clever skewers for these shrimp kabobs. You can serve this as an appetizer or as a main course.

seafood appetizer balls

1 can (6 ounces) crabmeat, drained, flaked and cartilage removed

¾ cup seasoned bread crumbs, *divided*

¼ cup finely chopped celery

¼ cup frozen cooked tiny shrimp, thawed

1 egg, lightly beaten

1 green onion, sliced

1 tablespoon chopped sweet red pepper

1 tablespoon milk

1 teaspoon garlic powder

½ teaspoon dried parsley flakes

½ teaspoon seafood seasoning

½ teaspoon pepper

1 cup crushed butter-flavored crackers (about 25 crackers)

1 egg white, lightly beaten

Oil for deep-fat frying

1 In a large mixing bowl, combine the crab, ¼ cup bread crumbs, celery, shrimp, egg, onion, red pepper, milk, garlic powder, parsley, seafood seasoning and pepper. Shape into 1-in. balls.

2 Place the cracker crumbs, egg white and remaining bread crumbs in separate shallow bowls. Roll balls in bread crumbs; dip in egg white, then roll in cracker crumbs.

3 In an electric skillet or deep-fat fryer, heat oil to 375°. Fry a few balls at a time for 1-2 minutes on each side or until golden brown. Drain on paper towels. Serve warm.

YIELD: 1½ DOZEN.

Helen McLain, Quinlan, Texas

After sampling a similar appetizer at a local restaurant, I went home to create my own. Family and friends like my version even better!

tempura chicken wings

15 whole chicken wings (about
   3 pounds)

1 cup cornstarch

3 eggs, lightly beaten

Oil for deep-fat frying

½ cup sugar

½ cup white vinegar

½ cup currant jelly

¼ cup soy sauce

3 tablespoons ketchup

2 tablespoons lemon juice

1 Cut chicken wings into three sections; discard wing tip section. Place cornstarch in a large resealable plastic bag; add chicken wings, a few at a time, and shake to coat evenly. Dip wings in eggs.

2 In an electric skillet or deep-fat fryer, heat oil to 375°. Fry wings for 8 minutes or until golden brown and juices run clear, turning occasionally. Drain on paper towels.

3 In a small saucepan, combine the sugar, vinegar, jelly, soy sauce, ketchup and lemon juice. Bring to a boil. Reduce heat; simmer, uncovered, for 10 minutes.

4 Place chicken wings in a greased 15-in. x 10-in. x 1-in. baking pan. Pour half of the sauce over wings. Bake, uncovered, at 350° for 15 minutes. Turn wings; top with remaining sauce. Bake 10-15 minutes longer or until chicken juices run clear and coating is set.

YIELD: 2½ DOZEN.

EDITOR'S NOTE: 3 pounds of uncooked chicken wing sections (wingettes) may be substituted for the whole chicken wings. Omit the first step.

Susan Wuckowitsch, Lenexa, Kansas

When I moved to Kansas City from Texas, I brought many of my mom's best-loved recipes with me, including these saucy, sweet-and-sour wings. This recipe turned a friend of mine, who's not a fan of chicken, into a real wing lover.

hearty ham balls

2 pounds ground fully cooked ham

1 pound ground beef

1 pound ground pork

2 cups graham cracker crumbs

2 egg, beaten

2/3 cup milk

1 can (10¾ ounces) condensed tomato soup, undiluted

½ cup packed brown sugar

2 to 4 tablespoons honey

2 tablespoons white vinegar

1 to 2 tablespoons ground mustard

1 In a large bowl, combine the ham, beef, pork, cracker crumbs, eggs and milk; mix well. Shape into 48 balls. Place in two greased 13-in. x 9-in. x 2-in. baking dishes.

2 Combine the remaining ingredients; pour over the ham balls. Bake, uncovered, at 350° for 45-50 minutes or until browned, basting the ham balls several times.

YIELD: 4 DOZEN.

Eulala Schwabac, Stanberry, Missouri

A very special lady shared this recipe with me. She asked me to make these ham balls when I cooked at her nursing home. Everyone enjoyed them there—and my family does, too.

toasty treats

150

142

No matter what the occasion, oven-fresh appetizers will disappear quickly when passed around. With variety to choose from, like Feta Artichoke B tes (p. 167), Bacon-Pecan Stuffed Mushrooms (p. 145) Spinach Squares (p. 150) or Cheese Boereg (p. 142) you're certain to find something that will appeal to your friends.

Just because these toasty treats take time to heat, don't hesitate to add them to your menu mix. Simply keep a tray warm in the oven or cook them in batches while you enjoy time with guests.

spinach-cheese mushroom caps

24 large fresh mushrooms

¼ cup chopped onion

2 garlic cloves, minced

1 tablespoon olive oil

1 package (8 ounces) cream cheese, softened

1 package (10 ounces) frozen chopped spinach, thawed and squeezed dry

½ cup plus 2 tablespoons shredded Parmesan cheese, *divided*

½ cup crumbled feta cheese

1 bacon strip, cooked and crumbled

½ teaspoon salt

1 Remove stems from mushrooms; set caps aside. Finely chop the stems. In a skillet, saute the chopped mushrooms, onion and garlic in oil until tender.

2 In a mixing bowl, beat cream cheese until smooth. Add the spinach, ½ cup Parmesan cheese, feta cheese, bacon, salt and mushroom mixture. Spoon into mushroom caps. Sprinkle with the remaining Parmesan cheese.

3 Place on a baking sheet. Bake at 400° for 15 minutes or until golden brown.

YIELD: 2 DOZEN.

Sandy Herman, Marietta, Georgia

Dainty finger foods like these mushrooms are a nice way to welcome guests into your home. A hearty spinach filling will tide folks over until the meal is served.

seasoned potato wedges

1/3 cup all-purpose flour

1/3 cup grated Parmesan cheese

1 teaspoon paprika

3 large baking potatoes (about 2 3/4 pounds)

1/3 cup milk

1/4 cup butter, *divided*

SOUR CREAM DIP:

2 cups (16 ounces) sour cream

8 bacon strips, cooked and crumbled

2 tablespoons minced chives

1/2 teaspoon garlic powder

1 In a large resealable plastic bag, combine the flour, Parmesan cheese and paprika. Cut each potato into eight wedges; dip in milk. Place in the bag, a few at a time, and shake to coat.

2 Place potatoes on a greased 15-in. x 10-in. x 1-in. baking pan. Drizzle with 2 tablespoons butter. Bake, uncovered, at 400° for 20 minutes.

3 Turn wedges; drizzle with remaining butter. Bake 20-25 minutes longer or until potatoes are tender and golden brown.

4 In a large bowl, combine dip ingredients. Serve with warm potato wedges.

YIELD: 6-8 SERVINGS.

Karen Trewin, Decorah, Iowa

These baked wedges, seasoned with Parmesan cheese and served with a sour cream dip, make a nice alternative to french fries or baked potatoes. They go great with grilled steak, but my family enjoys them as snacks, too.

cheese boereg

Jean Ecos, Hartland, Wisconsin

This Armenian appetizer has a rich-tasting cheese filling, which is baked between buttery layers of phyllo dough.

1 egg, lightly beaten

1 egg white, lightly beaten

1 cup ricotta cheese

¼ cup minced fresh parsley

4 cups (16 ounces) shredded part-skim mozzarella *or* Muenster cheese

10 sheets phyllo dough (18 inches x 14 inches)

½ cup butter, melted

1 In a bowl, combine the egg, egg white, ricotta and parsley. Stir in mozzarella; set aside.

2 Unroll phyllo dough; cut stack of sheets in half widthwise. Place one sheet of phyllo dough in a greased 13-in. x 9-in. x 2-in. baking pan; brush with butter. Repeat nine times. Keep remaining dough covered with plastic wrap and a damp towel to prevent it from drying out.

3 Spread cheese mixture evenly over top. Layer with remaining dough, brushing butter on every other sheet.

4 Bake at 350° for 25-30 minutes or until golden brown. Cut into triangles or squares.

YIELD: 16-20 APPETIZER SERVINGS.

pizza poppers

4 to 4½ cups all-purpose flour

⅓ cup sugar

1 package (¼ ounce) active dry yeast

1 teaspoon dried oregano

½ teaspoon salt

1 cup water

1 tablespoon shortening

1 egg

3 cups (12 ounces) shredded part-skim mozzarella cheese

1⅓ cups minced pepperoni (about 5 ounces)

2 cups pizza sauce, warmed

1 In a large mixing bowl, combine 2 cups flour, sugar, yeast, oregano and salt. In a saucepan, heat water and shortening to 120°-130°. Add to dry ingredients; beat until moistened. Add egg; beat on medium speed for 1 minute. Stir in cheese and pepperoni; mix well. Stir in enough remaining flour to form a soft dough.

2 Turn onto a floured surface; knead until smooth and elastic, about 6-8 minutes. Place in a greased bowl, turning once to grease top. Cover and let rise in a warm place until doubled, about 1 hour.

3 Punch dough down. Turn onto a lightly floured surface; divide into four pieces. Divide each piece into eight balls. Roll each ball into a 12-in. rope. Tie into a loose knot, leaving two long ends. Fold top end under roll; bring bottom end up and press into center of roll. Place on greased baking sheets. Cover and let rise until doubled, about 30 minutes.

4 Bake at 375° for 10-12 minutes or until golden brown. Serve warm with pizza sauce.

YIELD: 32 APPETIZERS.

Denise Sargent, Pittsfield, New Hampshire

Both my husband and I are big pizza fans, so we created these pizza rolls. They'll go fast at any gathering.

bacon-pecan stuffed mushrooms

1 pound large fresh mushrooms

4 tablespoons butter, *divided*

2 tablespoons vegetable oil

¼ teaspoon salt

2 tablespoons finely chopped onion

1 cup soft bread crumbs

6 bacon strips, cooked and crumbled

2 tablespoons chopped pecans

2 tablespoons sherry *or* beef broth

2 tablespoons sour cream

2 tablespoons minced chives

1 Remove mushroom stems (discard or save for another use). In a large skillet, heat 2 tablespoons butter and oil over medium-high heat. Saute mushroom caps for 2 minutes on each side; sprinkle with salt. Remove with a slotted spoon to paper towels.

2 In the same skillet, saute the onion in remaining butter until tender. Remove from the heat; stir in the remaining ingredients.

3 Spoon into mushroom caps. Place on a broiler pan; broil 5 in. from the heat for 2-3 minutes or until filling is browned. Serve warm.

YIELD: 12-14 APPETIZERS.

Beverly Pierce, Indianola, Mississippi
When I had some kitchen remodeling done a few years ago, this recipe disappeared. But I'd shared it so often that I had no trouble getting a copy.

cheddar artichoke quiche cups

2 jars (7½ ounces *each*) marinated artichoke hearts

1 small onion, finely chopped

1 garlic clove, minced

4 eggs, beaten

¼ cup dry bread crumbs

¼ teaspoon ground mustard

⅛ teaspoon dried oregano

⅛ teaspoon pepper

⅛ teaspoon hot pepper sauce

2 cups (8 ounce) shredded cheddar cheese

2 tablespoons minced fresh parsley

1 Drain artichokes, reserving half of the marinade. Chop artichokes; set aside. In a skillet, saute onion and garlic in reserved marinade until tender; set aside.

2 In a large bowl, combine the egg, bread crumbs, mustard, oregano, pepper and hot pepper sauce. Stir in the cheese, parsley, reserved artichokes and onion mixture.

3 Fill miniature muffin cups three-fourths full. Bake at 325° for 15-17 minutes or until set. Cool for 5 minutes before removing from pan to wire racks. Serve warm. Refrigerate leftovers.

YIELD: 4 DOZEN.

Fran Dell, Las Vegas, Nevada

No one can resist sampling these savory bites chock-full of artichokes, onions and cheese. They're at the top of my family's list for every holiday gathering. And whether I serve them hot or cold, there are never any left!

onion blossoms

2 large sweet onions, unpeeled

½ cup mayonnaise

½ cup sour cream

1 tablespoon chili powder

2½ teaspoons Cajun seasoning, *divided*

1¼ cups all-purpose flour

1 cup milk

Oil for deep-fat frying

1 Leaving the root end intact, peel the outer skin of the onion. Cut a small slice off the top. Starting at the top of the onion and on one side, make a cut downward toward the root end, stopping ½ in. from the bottom. Make additional cuts ⅛ in. from the first until there are cuts completely across top of onion.

2 Turn the onion a quarter turn so the slices are horizontal to you. Repeat the cuts ⅛ in. apart from each other until there is a checkerboard pattern across entire top of onion.

3 For dip, in a small bowl, combine the mayonnaise, sour cream, chili powder and 1/2 teaspoons Cajun seasoning. Mix well and set aside.

4 In a 1-gallon plastic bag, combine the flour and the remaining Cajun seasoning. Place milk in a small deep bowl. Coat the cut onion in flour, then dip into milk and back into the flour mixture.

5 Fry in enough oil to cover onion at 350° for 5 minutes or until golden, turning once. Remove from oil; place on serving plate. Discard the very center of the fried onion blossom. Place a few spoonful of dip in the center of blossom and serve immediately.

YIELD: 4 APPETIZER SERVINGS.

Jeanne Bennett, Minden, Louisiana

Onion blossoms are a popular appetizer served at many restaurants. Now you can easily make them at home with this delicious recipe.

sausage cheese squares

1 tube (8 ounces) refrigerated crescent rolls

1 package (8 ounces) brown-and-serve sausage links, thawed and sliced 1/2 inch thick

2 cups (8 ounces) shredded Monterey Jack cheese

4 eggs

3/4 cup milk

2 tablespoons chopped green pepper

1/2 teaspoon salt

1/4 teaspoon pepper

1 Unroll dough; place in an ungreased 13-in. x 9-in. x 2-in. baking dish. Press onto bottom and 1/2 in. up sides to form a crust. Top with sausage and cheese. Beat eggs in a bowl; add remaining ingredients. Carefully pour over cheese.

2 Bake, uncovered, at 425° for 20-25 minutes or until a knife inserted near the center comes out clean. Cut into small squares.

YIELD: 12-16 SERVINGS.

Helen McFadden, Sierra Vista, Arizona

My grandsons tried these savory morsels for the first time as youngsters and loved them. Though they're all grown up now, the boys still request the squares—and I'm happy to oblige!

deep-fried potato skins

4 large baking potatoes

2 cups (16 ounces) sour cream

1 envelope onion soup mix

1 tablespoon finely chopped onion

5 garlic cloves, minced

Dash hot pepper sauce

Oil for deep-fat frying

½ cup shredded cheddar cheese

½ cup shredded Swiss cheese

6 to 8 bacon strips, cooked and crumbled

4 teaspoons minced chives *or* green onion

1 Bake potatoes at 400° for 1 hour or until tender.

2 Meanwhile, for dip, combine the sour cream, soup mix, onion, garlic and hot pepper sauce in a bowl. Cover and refrigerate until serving.

3 When potatoes are cool enough to handle, cut in half lengthwise. Scoop out pulp, leaving a ¼-in. shell (save pulp for another use). With a scissors, cut each potato half into three lengthwise strips.

4 In an electric skillet or deep-fat fryer, heat oil to 375°. Fry skins in oil for 2-3 minutes or until golden brown and crisp.

5 Place potato skins in a 15-in. x 10-in. x 1-in. baking pan. Combine the cheeses and bacon; sprinkle over potatoes. Broil 4 in. from the heat for 1-2 minutes or until cheese is melted. Sprinkle with chives. Serve with the dip.

YIELD: 2 DOZEN.

Leslie Cunnian, Peterborough, Ontario

The combination of potatoes, cheese, bacon and garlic dip in this recipe is fantastic. The skins can be served as an appetizer or as a side dish with roast prime rib or any other entree you choose.

spinach squares

Patricia Kile, Greentown, Pennsylvania

Even people who don't care for spinach can't pass up these satisfying squares when they're set out.

2 tablespoons butter, *divided*

1 cup milk

3 eggs

1 cup all-purpose flour

1 teaspoon baking powder

¾ teaspoon salt

½ teaspoon dried oregano

¼ teaspoon pepper

¼ teaspoon dried basil

¼ teaspoon dried thyme

2 packages (10 ounces *each*) frozen chopped spinach, thawed and squeezed dry

2 cups (8 ounces) shredded cheddar cheese

2 cups (8 ounces) shredded Monterey Jack cheese

1 cup chopped onion

Sliced pimientos, optional

1 Brush the bottom and sides of a 13-in. x 9-in. x 2-in. baking dish with 1 tablespoon butter; set aside. In a large mixing bowl, combine the remaining butter and the next nine ingredients. Stir in the spinach, cheeses and onion.

2 Spread in pan. Bake, uncovered, at 350° for 30-35 minutes or until a toothpick inserted near the center comes out clean and edges are lightly browned. Cut into squares. Garnish with pimientos if desired.

YIELD: 4 DOZEN.

prosciutto puffs

1 cup water

6 tablespoons butter

1/8 teaspoon pepper

1 cup all-purpose flour

5 eggs

3/4 cup finely chopped prosciutto *or* fully cooked ham

1/4 cup minced chives

1 In a large saucepan, bring the water, butter and pepper to a boil. Add flour all at once and stir until a smooth ball forms. Remove from the heat; let stand for 5 minutes.

2 Add eggs, one at a time, beating well after each addition. Continue beating until mixture is smooth and shiny. Stir in prosciutto and chives.

3 Drop by heaping teaspoonfuls onto greased baking sheets. Bake at 425° for 18-22 minutes or until golden brown. Remove to wire racks. Serve warm. Refrigerate leftovers.

YIELD: 4 1/2 DOZEN.

Nella Parker, Hersey, Michigan

Your guests will come back for seconds and even thirds of these light and tasty puffs. They're so delicious that they practically melt in your mouth.

tater-dipped veggies

1 cup instant potato flakes

1/3 cup grated Parmesan cheese

1/2 teaspoon celery salt

1/4 teaspoon garlic powder

1/4 cup butter, melted and cooled

2 eggs

4 to 5 cups raw bite-size vegetables
(mushrooms, peppers, broccoli,
cauliflower, zucchini *and/or*
parboiled carrots)

Prepared ranch salad dressing *or* dip,
optional

1 In a small bowl, combine the potato flakes, Parmesan cheese, celery salt, garlic powder and butter. In another bowl, beat eggs. Dip vegetables, one at a time, into egg, then into potato mixture; coat well.

2 Place on an ungreased baking sheet. Bake at 400° for 20-25 minutes. Serve with dressing or dip if desired.

YIELD: 6-8 SERVINGS.

Earleen Lillegard, Prescott, Arizona

Deep-fried vegetables are terrific, but it's not always convenient to prepare them for company. Here's a recipe that produces the same deliciously crisp results in the oven. Serve with your favorite ranch-style dressing as a dip.

fried corn balls

1 egg, lightly beaten

1 can (8¼ ounces) cream-style corn

¾ cup crushed saltines (about 22 crackers)

½ teaspoon sugar

½ teaspoon baking powder

Oil for deep-fat frying

1 In a bowl, combine the first five ingredients to form a soft batter.

2 In an electric skillet or deep-fat fryer, heat oil to 375°. Drop batter by rounded teaspoonfuls; fry until golden brown, about 1 minute on each side. Drain on paper towels. Serve warm.

YIELD: ABOUT 2 DOZEN.

Ronnie-Ellen Timoner, Middletown, New York

These bite-size treats are so easy to make. Serve them as an appetizer or as a side to a beef or chicken entree.

bacon water chestnut wraps

1 pound sliced bacon

2 cans (8 ounces *each*) whole water chestnuts, drained

½ cup packed brown sugar

½ cup mayonnaise

¼ cup chili sauce

1 Cut bacon strips in half. In a skillet over medium heat, cook bacon until almost crisp; drain. Wrap each bacon piece around a water chestnut and secure with a toothpick. Place in an ungreased 13-in. x 9-in. x 2-in. baking dish.

2 Combine the brown sugar, mayonnaise and chili sauce; pour over water chestnuts. Bake, uncovered, at 350° for 30 minutes or until hot and bubbly.

YIELD: ABOUT 2½ DOZEN.

Laura Mahaffey, Annapolis, Maryland

The holidays around the house just wouldn't be the same without these classic wraps. Through the years, Christmas Eve guests have proved it's impossible to eat just one.

tomato leek tarts

1 package (15 ounces) refrigerated pie pastry

4 ounces provolone cheese, shredded

1 pound leeks (white portion only), sliced

6 medium plum tomatoes, thinly sliced

¼ cup grated Parmesan cheese

1½ teaspoons garlic powder

⅛ teaspoon pepper

1 cup (8 ounces) shredded part-skim mozzarella cheese

1 Place both pastry sheets on creased baking sheets. Sprinkle each with provolone cheese, leaving 1 in. around edges. Arrange leeks and tomato slices over provolone cheese. Sprinkle with Parmesan cheese, garlic powder and pepper. Top with mozzarella cheese. Fold edges over filling.

2 Bake at 425° for 18-22 minutes or until crusts are lightly browned. Cut into wedges. Serve warm.

YIELD: 2 TARTS.

Kathleen Tribble, Santa Ynez, California

You'll get two attractive, rustic-looking tarts from this delicious recipe. The crisp pastry crust cuts easily into wedges.

spinach spirals with mushroom sauce

¾ pound fresh mushrooms, sliced

¼ cup butter

3 tablespoons all-purpose flour

1 cup chicken broth

1 cup half-and-half cream

2 tablespoons sherry *or* additional chicken broth

1 teaspoon Dijon mustard

½ teaspoon lemon juice

SPINACH ROLL:

½ cup dry bread crumbs

3 packages (10 ounces *each*) frozen chopped spinach, thawed and squeezed dry

6 tablespoons butter, melted

¼ teaspoon salt

⅛ teaspoon pepper

⅛ teaspoon ground nutmeg

4 eggs, *separated*

¼ cup grated Parmesan cheese

1 In a large skillet, saute mushrooms in butter for 2-3 minutes. Stir in flour until blended; cook 2-3 minutes longer or until liquid is absorbed. Gradually stir in broth and cream. Bring to a boil. Remove from the heat; stir in the sherry or additional broth, mustard and lemon juice. Cool for 15 minutes.

2 Line a greased 15-in. x 10-in. x 1-in. baking pan with parchment paper; grease the paper. Sprinkle with bread crumbs; set aside. In a large bowl, combine the spinach, butter, salt, pepper, nutmeg and egg yolks. In a small mixing bowl, beat egg whites on high speed until stiff peaks form. Gradually fold into spinach mixture. Gently spoon over bread crumbs; press down lightly. Sprinkle with Parmesan cheese.

3 Bake at 350° for 12-15 minutes or until center springs back when lightly touched. Cover with a piece of greased foil; immediately invert pan onto foil. Gently peel away parchment paper.

4 Spread 1 cup mushroom sauce over spinach mixture to within 1 in. of edges. Roll up jelly-roll style, starting with a short side and peeling foil away while rolling. Cut into slices. Reheat remaining mushroom sauce; serve with spinach spirals.

YIELD: 12 SERVINGS.

Mrs. Archie Potts, San Antonio, Texas
I never thought I liked spinach until I tried these pretty spirals topped with a creamy mushroom sauce! It is a delicious dish to serve at a festive gathering.

fried cheese nuggets

½ cup dry bread crumbs

1 tablespoon sesame seeds

2 eggs, lightly beaten

1 package (10 ounces) extra-sharp cheddar cheese

Oil for deep-fat frying

1 In a shallow bowl, combine bread crumbs and sesame seeds. Place eggs in another shallow bowl. Cut cheese into ¾-in. cubes; dip in eggs, then coat with crumb mixture. Refrigerate for 15 minutes or until coating is set.

2 In an electric skillet or deep-fat fryer, heat 1 in. oil to 375°. Fry cheese cubes for 1-2 minutes or until browned. Drain on paper towels. Serve warm.

YIELD: 2 DOZEN.

Pat Waymire, Yellow Springs, Ohio

There's just something about cheese that folks can't resist, and these cheese nuggets are no exception. I barely finish making a batch before they disappear!

bacon-wrapped scallops

20 fresh baby spinach leaves

10 uncooked sea scallops, halved

10 bacon strips, halved widthwise

Lemon wedges

1 Fold a spinach leaf around each scallop half. Wrap bacon over spinach and secure with a toothpick. Place on baking sheet or broiler pan.

2 Broil 3-4 in. from the heat for 6 minutes on each side or until bacon is crisp and scallops are opaque. Squeeze lemon over each. Serve immediately.

YIELD: 20 APPETIZERS.

Pamela MacCumbee, Berkeley Springs, West Virginia

When I'm looking for more special appetizer, this is the recipe I reach for. I've also served these savory scallops for dinner.

italian garlic breadsticks

Taste of Home Test Kitchen

A seasoned Parmesan cheese coating gives refrigerated breadsticks a terrific taste twist. The wonderful aroma of these breadsticks baking is so irresistible, you just may need to make another batch!

½ cup grated Parmesan cheese

2 teaspoons Italian seasoning

1 teaspoon garlic powder

¼ cup butter, melted

1 tube (11 ounces) refrigerated breadsticks

1 In a shallow bowl, combine the cheese, Italian seasoning and garlic powder. Place butter in another shallow bowl. Separate dough into individual breadsticks. Dip in butter, then in cheese mixture. Twist 2-3 times and place on an ungreased baking sheet.

2 Bake at 375° for 12-14 minutes or until golden brown. Serve immediately.

YIELD: 1 DOZEN.

clam-stuffed mushrooms

24 large fresh mushrooms

2 cans (6½ ounces *each*) minced clams, drained

¾ cup dry bread crumbs

½ cup grated Parmesan cheese

½ cup finely chopped green pepper

1 small onion, finely chopped

2 garlic cloves, minced

2 tablespoons Italian seasoning

2 tablespoons dried parsley flakes

⅛ teaspoon pepper

1½ cups butter, melted, *divided*

½ cup shredded part-skim mozzarella cheese

1 Remove mushroom stems (discard or save for another use); set caps aside. In a large bowl, combine the clams, bread crumbs, Parmesan cheese, green pepper, onion, garlic, Italian seasoning, parsley and pepper. Stir in ¾ cup butter. Fill each mushroom cap with about 1 tablespoon clam mixture.

2 Place in an ungreased 15-in. x 10-in. x 1-in. baking pan. Sprinkle with mozzarella cheese; drizzle with remaining butter. Bake, uncovered, at 350° for 20-25 minutes or until lightly browned. Serve warm.

YIELD: 2 DOZEN.

Maria Regakis, Somerville, Massachusetts

Seafood lovers will savor these tasty bites. Mushroom caps are stuffed with a pleasing combination of minced clams, cheese and seasonings.

blue cheese crostini

4 ounces cream cheese, softened

3 tablespoons butter, softened

1 cup (4 ounces) crumbled blue cheese

¼ cup finely chopped walnuts, toasted

15 slices French bread (½ inch thick), lightly toasted

1 medium ripe pear

1 In a small mixing bowl, beat cream cheese and butter until smooth. Stir in the blue cheese and walnuts Spread evenly over toasted bread.

2 Place on a baking sheet. Broil 3-4 in. from the heat for 3-4 minutes or until cheese is bubbly. Core pear and cut into 30 thin slices. Place two pear slices on each crostini. Serve warm.

YIELD: 15 APPETIZERS.

Kate Hilts, Grand Rapids, Michigan

My sister-in-law gave me this great recipe, which includes two of my favorite ingredients—blue cheese and pears. Yum!

bacon nachos

½ pound ground beef

4 cups tortilla chips

¼ cup real bacon bits

2 cups (8 ounces) shredded cheddar cheese

½ cup guacamole dip

½ cup sour cream

Chopped tomatoes and green onions, optional

1 In a small skillet, cook beef over medium heat until no longer pink; drain. Place the tortilla chips on a microwave-safe serving plate. Layer with the beef, bacon and cheese.

2 Microwave, uncovered, on high for 1-2 minutes or until cheese is melted. Top with guacamole and sour cream. Sprinkle with the tomatoes and onions if desired.

YIELD: 4-6 SERVINGS.

EDITOR'S NOTE: This recipe was tested in a 1,100-watt microwave.

Ruth Ann Bott, Lake Wales, Florida

These crispy nachos have always been a big hit in our house. Topped with kid-friendly ingredients like ground beef and cheddar cheese, they're sure to be requested by your children.

crunchy onion sticks

2 eggs, lightly beaten

2 tablespoons butter, melted

1 teaspoon all-purpose flour

½ teaspoon garlic salt

½ teaspoon dried parsley flakes

¼ teaspoon onion salt

2 cans (2.8 ounces *each*) french-fried onions, crushed

1 tube (8 ounces) refrigerated crescent rolls

1 In a shallow bowl, combine the first six ingredients. Place the onions in another shallow bowl. Separate crescent dough into four rectangles; seal perforations. Cut each rectangle into eight strips. Dip each strip in egg mixture, then roll in onions.

2 Place 2 in. apart on ungreased baking sheets. Bake at 375° for 10-12 minutes or until golden brown. Immediately remove from baking sheets. Serve warm.

YIELD: 32 APPETIZERS.

Leora Muellerleile, Turtle Lake, Wisconsin

Although I've been collecting recipes for more than 50 years, I never tire of tried-and-true ones like this.

crab puffs

1 cup plus 1 tablespoon water

½ cup butter

1 tablespoon ground mustard

1 teaspoon salt

1 teaspoon ground cumin

⅛ teaspoon hot pepper sauce

1 cup all-purpose flour

4 eggs

2 cups (8 ounces) shredded Swiss cheese

1 can (6 ounces) crabmeat, drained, flaked and cartilage removed

1 In a large saucepan, bring the water, butter, mustard, salt, cumin and hot pepper sauce to a boil. Add flour all at once and stir until a smooth ball forms. Remove from the heat; let stand for 5 minutes.

2 Add eggs, one at a time, beating well after each addition. Continue beating until smooth and shiny. Stir in the cheese and crab.

3 Drop by rounded teaspoonfuls 2 in. apart onto greased baking sheets. Bake at 400° for 23-26 minutes or until golden brown. Remove to wire racks. Serve warm.

YIELD: ABOUT 4 DOZEN.

Nadia Miheyev, Richmond Hill, New York

If you're looking for a scrumptious way to get a party started, bring out a tray of these cheesy crab puffs. They bake up golden brown and taste wonderful right out of the oven. Try serving them with soup.

fried onion rings

1 large Vidalia *or* sweet onion

¾ cup all-purpose flour

¼ cup cornmeal

½ teaspoon baking powder

½ teaspoon salt

¼ teaspoon baking soda

¼ teaspoon cayenne pepper

1 egg

1 cup buttermilk

Oil for deep-fat frying

LIME DIPPING SAUCE:

⅔ cup mayonnaise

3 tablespoons honey

2 tablespoons lime juice

2 tablespoons spicy brown *or* horseradish mustard

1 teaspoon prepared horseradish

1 Cut onion into ½-in. slices; separate into rings. In a bowl, combine the flour, cornmeal, baking powder, salt, baking soda and cayenne. Combine the egg and buttermilk stir into dry ingredients just until moistened.

2 In an electric skillet or deep-fat fryer, heat 1 in. of oil to 375°. Dip onion rings into batter. Fry a few at a time for 1 to 1½ minutes on each side or until golden brown. Drain on paper towels (keep warm in a 300° oven).

3 In a small bowl, combine sauce ingredients. Serve with onion rings.

YIELD: 4 SERVINGS.

Christine Wilson, Sellersville, Pennsylvania

Sweet Vidalia onion rings are deep-fried to a crispy golden brown, then served with a cool and zesty lime dipping sauce.

jalapeno poppers

2 jars (11½ ounces *each*) jalapeno peppers

1 package (8 ounces) cream cheese, softened

1 cup (4 ounces) shredded cheddar cheese

¼ cup grated Parmesan cheese

1 tablespoon dried parsley flakes

2 teaspoons garlic salt

2 teaspoons paprika

¼ cup all-purpose flour

3 eggs

1 cup crushed cornflakes

½ cup dry bread crumbs

Oil for frying

SAUCE:

¼ cup mayonnaise

¼ cup prepared Russian salad dressing

1 teaspoon prepared horseradish

1 teaspoon dried parsley flakes

½ teaspoon pepper

¼ teaspoon salt

Dash Louisiana-style hot sauce

1 Select 12-16 large jalapenos from jars; pat dry with paper towels (refrigerate any remaining jalapenos for another use). Remove stems from jalapenos; cut a lengthwise slit on one side. Discard seeds. In a small mixing bowl, combine the cheeses, parsley, garlic salt and paprika. Pipe or stuff into each pepper.

2 Place flour in a shallow bowl. In another shallow bowl, lightly beat the eggs. In a separate bowl, combine cornflakes and bread crumbs. Roll jalapenos in flour, dip in eggs, then roll in crumbs. Dip again in eggs, then roll in crumbs to completely coat.

3 In an electric skillet, heat ¼ in. of oil to 375°. Fry peppers, a few at a time, for 30-60 seconds or until lightly browned. Drain on paper towels. In a small bowl, combine sauce ingredients. Serve with warm peppers.

YIELD: 12-16 APPETIZERS.

EDITOR'S NOTE: When cutting or seeding hot peppers, use rubber or plastic gloves to protect your hands. Avoid touching your face.

James Brophy, Feasterville Trevose, Pennsylvania

After sampling similar poppers at a wedding reception, I went home to create my own recipe. The creamy filling pairs well with the spicy peppers.

potato nachos

8 medium red potatoes

1 envelope ranch salad dressing mix

1 jar (12 ounces) pickled jalapeno pepper slices, drained

2 cups (8 ounces) shredded cheddar cheese

2 cups (8 ounces) shredded Monterey Jack cheese

2 cups (16 ounces) sour cream

6 to 8 green onions, chopped

1 Place potatoes in a saucepan and cover with water. Bring to a boil. Reduce heat; cover and cook for 15-20 minutes or just until tender. Drain; cool slightly.

2 Cut potatoes into ¼-in.-thick slices. Place in a single layer in three greased 15-in. x 10-in. x 1-in. baking pans. Top each with salad dressing mix, a jalapeno slice, cheddar cheese and Monterey Jack cheese.

3 Bake, uncovered, at 350° for 10-12 minutes or until cheese is melted. Top with sour cream and green onions.

YIELD: 12 SERVINGS.

Tony Horton, Van Buren, Arkansas

Cheese, jalapeno pepper, sour cream and green onions top these pretty potato slices, seasoned with dry ranch dressing mix. I love to serve them to guests, and they love to eat them. You can use them as an appetizer or even as a side dish.

feta artichoke bites

1 jar (7½ ounces) marinated artichoke hearts

1 cup diced seeded tomatoes

1 cup (4 ounces) crumbled feta cheese

⅓ cup grated Parmesan cheese

2 green onions, thinly sliced

1 loaf sourdough baguette (about 20 inches long)

1 Drain artichokes, reserving 2 tablespoons marinade. Chop artichokes and place in a large bowl. Stir in the tomatoes, cheeses, onions and reserved marinade. Cover and refrigerate for 1 hour.

2 Cut baguette into ½-in. slices. Spread with artichoke mixture. Place on an ungreased baking sheet. Broil 4-6 in. from the heat for 4-5 minutes or until edges of bread are browned. Serve immediately.

YIELD: ABOUT 12 SERVINGS

Louise Leach, Chino, California

You can prepare the flavorful topping for this appetizer ahead of time. Then spread onto slices of bread and broil for a fast, festive snack.

baked potato skins

4 large baking potatoes, baked

3 tablespoons vegetable oil

1 tablespoon grated Parmesan cheese

½ teaspoon salt

¼ teaspoon garlic powder

¼ teaspoon paprika

⅛ teaspoon pepper

8 bacon strips, cooked and crumbled

1½ cups (6 ounces) shredded cheddar cheese

½ cup sour cream

4 green onions, sliced

1 Cut potatoes in half lengthwise; scoop out pulp, leaving a ¼-in. shell (save pulp for another use). Place potato skins on a greased baking sheet. Combine the oil, Parmesan cheese, salt, garlic powder, paprika and pepper; brush over both sides of skins.

2 Bake at 475° for 7 minutes; turn. Bake until crisp, about 7 minutes longer. Sprinkle bacon and cheddar cheese inside skins. Bake for 2 minutes or until the cheese is melted. Top with sour cream and onions. Serve immediately.

YIELD: 8 SERVINGS.

Trish Perrin, Keizer, Oregon

Both crisp and hearty, this snack's one that is often requested by my family.

chicken nut puffs

1½ cups finely chopped cooked chicken

⅓ cup chopped almonds, toasted

1 cup chicken broth

½ cup vegetable oil

2 teaspoons Worcestershire sauce

1 tablespoon dried parsley flakes

1 teaspoon seasoned salt

½ to 1 teaspoon celery seed

⅛ teaspoon cayenne pepper

1 cup all-purpose flour

4 eggs

1 Combine the chicken and almonds; set aside. In a saucepan, combine the next seven ingredients; bring to a boil. Add flour all at once; stir until a smooth ball forms. Remove from the heat; let stand for 5 minutes.

2 Add eggs, one at a time, beating well after each. Beat until smooth. Stir in chicken and almonds.

3 Drop by heaping teaspoonfuls onto greased baking sheets. Bake at 450° for 12-14 minutes or until golden brown. Serve warm.

YIELD: ABOUT 6 DOZEN.

Jo Groth, Plainfield, Iowa
Of the 15 to 20 items I set out when hosting holiday parties, these savory puffs are the first to get snapped up. People enjoy the zippy flavor. They're a nice finger food to eat since they're not sticky or drippy.

shrimp puffs

2 eggs, *separated*

¾ cup milk

1 tablespoon vegetable oil

1 cup all-purpose flour

1½ teaspoons baking powder

1½ teaspoons onion powder

1 teaspoon salt

½ teaspoon pepper

3 cups cooked rice

1 pound uncooked shrimp, peeled, deveined and chopped *or* 2 cans (4½ ounces *each*) small shrimp, drained

¼ cup minced fresh parsley

½ teaspoon hot pepper sauce

Oil for deep-fat frying

1 In a large bowl, beat the egg yolks, milk and oil. Combine the flour, baking powder, onion powder, salt and pepper; add to yolk mixture and mix well. Stir in the rice, shrimp, parsley and hot pepper sauce.

2 In a mixing bowl, beat the egg whites until soft peaks form; fold into shrimp mixture.

3 In an electric skillet or deep-fat fryer, heat oil to 350°. Drop batter by tablespoons into hot oil. Fry puffs, a few at a time, for 1½ minutes on each side or until browned and puffy. Drain on paper towels. Serve warm.

YIELD: ABOUT 4 DOZEN.

Maudry Ramsey, Sulphur, Louisiana

Shrimp and rice are two foods that are abundant in our area. These shrimp puffs are my family's favorite.

calico clams casino

3 cans (6½ ounces *each*) minced clams

1 cup (4 ounces) shredded part-skim mozzarella cheese

1 cup (4 ounces) shredded cheddar cheese

4 bacon strips, cooked and crumbled

3 tablespoons seasoned bread crumbs

3 tablespoons butter, melted

2 tablespoons *each* finely chopped onion, celery and sweet red, yellow and green peppers

1 garlic clove, minced

Dash dried parsley flakes

1 Drain clams, reserving 2 tablespoons clam juice. In a large bowl, combine the clams and all the remaining ingredients; stir in the reserved clam juice. Spoon into greased 6-oz. custard cups or clamshell dishes; place on baking sheets

2 Bake at 350° for 10-15 minutes or until heated through and lightly browned.

YIELD: 8 SERVINGS.

Paula Sullivan, Barker, New York

A few years ago, I came across this recipe in the back of my files when I was looking for a special appetizer. Everyone raved about it. Now it's an often-requested dish.

creamy herb slices

1 package (8 ounces) cream cheese, softened

1 tablespoon minced fresh parsley

1 tablespoon minced chives

2 teaspoons chopped green onions

2 garlic cloves, minced

1 teaspoon dill weed

½ teaspoon pepper

1 loaf (½ pound) French bread

In a small bowl, combine the first seven ingredients. Cut bread into ½-in. slices; spread each slice with 1 tablespoon cream cheese mixture. Place on ungreased baking sheets. Bake at 400° for 7 minutes or broil for 2 minutes until golden brown.

YIELD: ABOUT 22 APPETIZERS.

Kelly Schulz, Oak Lawn, Illinois

These dressed-up slices of French bread go well with soup or salad, or can be served as an appetizer. I have to move fast after putting them out—or there are none left for me!

onion tart

1 unbaked pastry shell (9 inches)

2 medium sweet onions, thinly sliced

2 tablespoons olive oil

3 eggs

½ cup crumbled feta cheese

½ teaspoon salt

¼ teaspoon coarsely ground pepper

⅛ teaspoon ground nutmeg

⅛ teaspoon hot pepper sauce

¾ cup half-and-half cream

½ cup milk

1 tablespoon Dijon mustard

6 green onions, thinly sliced

2 tablespoons minced chives

⅓ cup grated Parmesan cheese

1 Line unpricked pastry shell with a double thickness of heavy-duty foil. Bake at 450° for 8 minutes. Remove foil; bake 5 minutes longer. Cool on a wire rack.

2 In a small skillet, saute the onions in oil until tender; cool. In a food processor, combine the eggs, feta cheese, salt, pepper, nutmeg and hot pepper sauce; cover and process until smooth. Gradually add cream and milk; process until blended.

3 Brush the inside of crust with mustard. Sprinkle the green onions, chives and sauteed onions over crust. Carefully pour egg mixture over onions. Sprinkle with Parmesan cheese.

4 Bake at 375° for 30-40 minutes or until a knife inserted near the center comes out clean. Let stand for 10 minutes before cutting. Serve warm.

YIELD: 6 SERVINGS.

Christine Andreas, Huntingdon, Pennsylvania
Onion lovers are sure to be asking for second helpings of this appetizing tart—it uses two kinds of onions! Parmesan and feta cheese, nutmeg and hot pepper sauce enhance the flavor nicely. With its quiche-like filling, the dish is ideal for a brunch or buffet.

crab-stuffed cherry tomatoes

1 pint cherry tomatoes

1 can (6 ounces) crabmeat, drained, flaked and cartilage removed

½ cup diced green pepper

2 green onions, diced

2 tablespoons Italian-seasoned bread crumbs

1 teaspoon white wine vinegar

½ teaspoon dried parsley flakes

¼ teaspoon dill weed

⅛ teaspoon salt, optional

1 Cut a thin slice off tops of tomatoes and carefully scoop out insides; invert on paper towels to drain In a small bowl, combine remaining ingredients; mix well.

2 Stuff tomatoes; place in an ungreased 13-in. x 9-in. x 2-in. baking dish. Bake, uncovered, at 350° for 8-10 minutes or until heated through. Serve warm.

YIELD: ABOUT 1½ DOZEN.

Marcia Keckhaver, Burlington, Wisconsin
For a little something special, I include these delicious, petite pleasers on the menu of our holiday parties.

cajun canapes

Jerri Peachee, Gentry, Arkansas

I came across these filled biscuits at a party—and now they're a family-favorite snack.

2 tubes (12 ounces *each*) refrigerated buttermilk biscuits

1/2 pound bulk pork sausage, cooked and drained

1 1/2 cups (6 ounces) shredded cheddar cheese

1/4 cup chopped green pepper

1/4 cup mayonnaise

2 green onions, chopped

2 teaspoons lemon juice

1/2 teaspoon salt

1/2 teaspoon paprika

1/4 teaspoon garlic powder

1/4 teaspoon dried thyme

1/8 to 1/4 teaspoon cayenne pepper

1 Bake biscuits according to package directions, except turn biscuits over halfway through baking. Remove from pans to wire racks to cool completely.

2 Using a melon baller, scoop out the center of each biscuit, leaving a 3/8-in. shell (discard biscuit center). In a bowl, combine the remaining ingredients. Spoon about 1 tablespoonful into the center of each biscuit.

3 Place on an ungreased baking sheet. Bake at 400° for 8-10 minutes or until heated through. Serve warm.

YIELD: 20 APPETIZERS.

veggie nachos

1 pound ground beef

2½ quarts water, *divided*

1 envelope taco seasoning

1 medium bunch broccoli, broken into small florets

1 medium head cauliflower, broken into small florets

1 package (15½ ounces) bite-size tortilla chips

1 can (11 ounces) condensed nacho cheese soup, undiluted

½ cup milk

¼ cup chopped sweet red pepper

1 can (2¼ ounces) sliced ripe olives, drained

1 In a skillet, cook beef over medium heat until no longer pink, drain. Add ¾ cup water and taco seasoning. Bring to a boil. Reduce heat; simmer, uncovered, for 15 minutes.

2 Meanwhile, in a large saucepan, bring remaining water to a boil. Add broccoli and cauliflower. Cook for 2 minutes; drain. Place chips on a large ovenproof serving platter. Top with beef mixture, broccoli and cauliflower. In a bowl, combine the soup, milk and red pepper. Drizzle over vegetables. Sprinkle with olives. Bake at 350° for 10 minutes or until heated through. Serve immediately.

YIELD: 12-16 SERVINGS.

Merry Holthus, Auburn, Nebraska
My family loves traditional nachos, but I was looking to offer something a little different. Now they gobble up this version with ground beef, vegetables and a creamy cheese sauce.

crisp caraway twists

1 egg

1 tablespoon water

1 teaspoon country-style Dijon mustard

¾ cup shredded Swiss cheese

¼ cup finely chopped onion

2 teaspoons minced fresh parsley

1½ teaspoons caraway seeds

¼ teaspoon garlic salt

1 sheet frozen puff pastry, thawed

1 In a small bowl, beat the egg, water and mustard; set aside. In another bowl, combine the cheese, onion, parsley, caraway seeds and garlic salt.

2 Unfold pastry sheet; brush with egg mixture. Sprinkle cheese mixture lengthwise over half of the pastry. Fold pastry over filling; press edges to seal. Brush top with remaining egg mixture. Cut widthwise into ½-in. strips; twist each strip several times.

3 Place 1 in. apart on greased baking sheets, pressing ends down. Bake at 350° for 15-20 minutes or until golden brown. Serve warm.

YIELD: ABOUT 1½ DOZEN.

Dorothy Smith, El Dorado, Arkansas

This appetizer is always a hit when I serve it on holidays or special occasions. The flaky cheese-filled twists—made with convenient puff pastry are baked to a crispy golden brown. When our big family gets together, I make two batches.

cheddar shrimp nachos

¾ pound deveined peeled cooked shrimp, chopped

1½ cups (6 ounces) shredded cheddar cheese

1 can (4 ounces) chopped green chilies, drained

⅓ cup chopped green onions

¼ cup sliced ripe olives, drained

½ cup mayonnaise

¼ teaspoon ground cumin

48 tortilla chip scoops

1 In a large bowl, combine the shrimp, cheese, chilies, onions and olives. Combine the mayonnaise and cumin; add to shrimp mixture and toss to coat.

2 Drop by tablespoonfuls into tortilla scoops. Place on ungreased baking sheets. Bake at 350° for 5-10 minutes or until cheese is melted. Serve warm.

YIELD: 4 DOZEN.

Lisa Feld, Grafton, Wisconsin
These fun finger foods in tortilla chip scoops are just the tasty thing for cold-weather get-togethers.

baked jalapenos

1 package (3 ounces) cream cheese, softened

¼ teaspoon ground cumin

⅔ cup shredded Monterey Jack cheese

1 teaspoon minced fresh cilantro

8 jalapeno peppers, halved lengthwise and seeded

1 egg, beaten

¾ cup cornflake crumbs

1 In a small mixing bowl, beat cream cheese and cumin until smooth. Beat in Monterey Jack cheese and cilantro. Spoon into jalapeno halves.

2 Place egg and cornflake crumbs in separate shallow bowls. Dip filling side of jalapenos in egg, then coat with crumbs. Place crumb side up on a greased baking sheet. Bake at 350° for 25-30 minutes or until top is golden brown. Serve immediately.

YIELD: 16 APPETIZERS.

EDITOR'S NOTE: When cutting or seeding hot peppers, use rubber or plastic gloves to protect your hands. Avoid touching your face.

Taste of Home Test Kitchen
This baked version of jalapeno poppers pairs a crunchy topping with a creamy filling.

cool nibbles

208

183

Chill out with easy appetizers you can plate before your party starts. Count on time-savers like Zesty Marinated Shrimp (p. 189), Savory Cheese Cutouts (p. 208) and Potato Salad Bites (p. 183).

For food-safe service, arrange appetizers on multiple plates. Then serve one plate while you keep the other refrigerated. Just refill as needed. Place a serving dish of items like shrimp or deviled eggs on a bed of ice for a presentation that's both practical and pretty.

ham 'n' cheese pinwheels

1 carton (8 ounces) whipped cream cheese

½ cup finely chopped walnuts

1 tablespoon ranch salad dressing mix

1 garlic clove, minced

9 thin slices deli ham

In a bowl, combine the cream cheese, walnuts, salad dressing mix and garlic. Spread about 2 tablespoons over each ham slice; roll up tightly and wrap in plastic wrap. Refrigerate for at least 2 hours. Unwrap; cut into 1-in. slices.

YIELD: ABOUT 4 DOZEN.

Andrea Bolden, Unionville, Tennessee

This recipe is a convenient make-ahead snack. I love the garlic flavor in these roll-ups. Every time I serve them, they're a hit.

potato salad bites

10 small red potatoes

¼ cup chopped pimiento-stuffed olives

 2 teaspoons minced fresh parsley

 1 teaspoon finely chopped onion

½ cup mayonnaise

1¾ teaspoons Dijon mustard

⅛ teaspoon pepper

¼ teaspoon salt

Paprika

Parsley sprigs, optional

1 Place the potatoes in a saucepan and cover with water. Bring to a boil. Reduce heat; cover and cook for 12-15 minutes or until tender. Drain and immediately place potatoes in ice water; drain and pat dry.

2 Peel two potatoes; finely dice and place in a small bowl. Cut the remaining potatoes in half. With a melon baller, scoop out pulp, leaving a 3/8-in. shell; set shells aside. Dice pulp and add to the bowl. Stir in the olives, parsley and onion. Combine the mayonnaise, mustard and pepper; gently stir into potato mixture.

3 Sprinkle potato shells with salt; stuff with potato salad. Sprinkle with paprika. Refrigerate for at least 1 hour before serving. Garnish with parsley if desired.

YIELD: 16 APPETIZERS.

Stephanie Sheridan, Plainfield, Vermont

Potatoes make the perfect platform for this colorful potato salad. They are just two or three bites, so you don't need a fork.

beef canapes with cucumber sauce

Taste of Home Test Kitchen

A homemade cucumber-yogurt sauce complements tender slices of beef in this recipe. Since both the meat and sauce are made in advance, this recipe requires very little last-minute preparation.

4 cups (32 ounces) plain yogurt

1 whole beef tenderloin (1½ pounds)

2 tablespoons olive oil, *divided*

1 teaspoon salt, *divided*

¼ teaspoon plus ⅛ teaspoon white pepper, *divided*

1 medium cucumber, peeled, seeded and diced

1 tablespoon finely chopped onion

1 garlic clove, minced

1 tablespoon white vinegar

1 (1 pound) French bread baguette, cut into 36 thin slices

1 cup fresh arugula

1 Line a fine mesh strainer with two layers of cheesecloth; place over a bowl. Place yogurt in strainer. Cover and refrigerate for at least 4 hours or overnight.

2 Rub tenderloin with 1 tablespoon oil. Sprinkle with ½ teaspoon salt and ¼ teaspoon white pepper. In a large skillet, cook the beef tenderloin over medium-high heat until browned on all sides. Transfer meat to a shallow roasting pan. Bake at 400° for 25-30 minutes or until a meat thermometer reads 145°. Cool on a wire rack for 1 hour. Cover and refrigerate.

3 Transfer yogurt from strainer to another bowl (discard yogurt liquid). Add the cucumber, onion, garlic and remaining salt and white pepper. In a small bowl, whisk the vinegar and remaining oil; stir into yogurt mixture.

4 Thinly slice tenderloin. Spread yogurt mixture over bread slices; top with beef and arugula. Serve immediately or cover and refrigerate until serving.

YIELD: 3 DOZEN.

artichoke crostini

1 sourdough baguette (1 pound)

2 cups chopped seeded tomatoes

1 can (14 ounces) water-packed artichoke hearts, rinsed, drained and chopped

2 tablespoons minced fresh basil

2 tablespoons olive oil

½ teaspoon seasoned salt

⅛ teaspoon pepper

1 Cut the baguette into 32 slices. Place on an ungreased baking sheet; spritz bread with nonstick cooking spray. Bake at 325° for 7-10 minutes or until crisp. Cool on a wire rack.

2 In a bowl, combine the tomatoes, artichokes, basil, oil, seasoned salt and pepper. Spoon onto bread slices.

YIELD: 32 APPETIZERS.

Janne Rowe, Wichita, Kansas

This appetizer is wonderful when vine-ripened tomatoes are at their best. I often rely on these fresh-tasting slices for parties and other events.

party puffs

1 cup water

½ cup butter

1 cup all-purpose flour

4 eggs

EGG SALAD FILLING:

6 hard-cooked eggs, chopped

⅓ cup mayonnaise

3 tablespoons chutney, finely chopped

2 green onions, finely chopped

1 teaspoon salt

½ teaspoon curry powder

HAM SALAD FILLING:

1 can (4¼ ounces) deviled ham

1 package (3 ounces) cream cheese, softened

2 tablespoons finely chopped green pepper

1½ teaspoons prepared horseradish

1 teaspoon lemon juice

1 In a saucepan over medium heat, bring water and butter to a boil. Add flour all at once and stir until a smooth ball forms. Remove from the heat; let stand for 5 minutes.

2 Add eggs, one at a time, beating well after each addition. Continue beating until mixture is smooth and shiny. Drop by teaspoonfuls 2 in. apart onto greased baking sheets.

3 Bake at 400° for 20-25 minutes or until lightly browned. Remove to wire racks. Immediately cut a slit in each puff to allow steam to escape; cool completely.

4 In separate bowls, combine the ingredients for egg salad filling and ham salad filling. Split puffs and remove soft dough from inside. Just before serving, spoon filling into puffs; replace tops. Refrigerate the leftovers.

YIELD: 7½ DOZEN.

Karen Owen, Rising Sun, Indiana

For a substantial appetizer, you can't go wrong with mini sandwiches. Instead of serving egg or ham salad on ordinary bread, I like to present them in homemade puff pastry.

antipasto platter

1 jar (32 ounces) pepperoncinis, drained

1 can (15 ounces) garbanzo beans *or* chickpeas, rinsed and drained

2 cups halved fresh mushrooms

2 cups halved cherry tomatoes

½ pound provolone cheese, cubed

1 can (6 ounces) pitted ripe olives, drained

1 package (3½ ounces) sliced pepperoni

1 bottle (8 ounces) Italian vinaigrette dressing

Lettuce leaves

In a large bowl, combine the peppers, beans, mushrooms, tomatoes, cheese, olives and pepperoni. Pour vinaigrette over mixture; toss to coat. Refrigerate for at least 30 minutes or overnight. Arrange on a lettuce-lined platter. Serve with toothpicks.

YIELD: 14-16 SERVINGS.

Teri Lindquist, Gurnee, Illinois

Here's a delicious change of pace from items you usually find on a buffet. We entertain often, and this one of our favorite party pleasers with family and friends.

zesty marinated shrimp

½ cup vegetable oil

½ cup lime juice

½ cup thinly sliced red onion

12 lemon slices

1 tablespoon minced fresh parsley

½ teaspoon salt

½ teaspoon dill weed

⅛ teaspoon hot pepper sauce

2 pounds medium shrimp, cooked, peeled and deveined

In a large bowl, combine the first eight ingredients. Stir in shrimp. Cover and refrigerate for 4 hours, stirring occasionally. Drain before serving.

YIELD: 12 SERVINGS.

Mary Jane Guest, Alamosa, Colorado

These easy shrimp look impressive on a buffet table and taste even better! The zesty sauce has a wonderful, spicy citrus flavor. I especially like this recipe because I can prepare it ahead of time.

marinated mushrooms

1 pound small fresh mushrooms

1 small onion, thinly sliced

⅓ cup white wine vinegar

⅓ cup vegetable oil

1 teaspoon salt

1 teaspoon ground mustard

In a large saucepan, combine all the ingredients. Bring to a boil over medium-high heat. Cook, uncovered, for 6 minutes, stirring once. Cool to room temperature. Transfer to a bowl; cover and refrigerate overnight.

YIELD: 3 CUPS.

Mark Curry, Buena Vista, Colorado

Add these flavorful mushrooms to an antipasto platter,

toss in a salad or just serve by themselves.

shrimp 'n' snow pea wrap-ups

1 cup oil and vinegar salad dressing

1 teaspoon minced fresh gingerroot

1 garlic clove, minced

1 pound cooked medium shrimp, peeled and deveined (about 36)

2 cups water

4 ounces fresh snow peas (about 36)

1 In a large bowl, combine the salad dressing, ginger and garlic. Stir in shrimp; cover and refrigerate for 2 hours.

2 Meanwhile, in a small saucepan, bring water to a boil. Add snow peas; cover and boil for 1 minute. Drain and immediately place peas in ice water; drain and pat dry.

3 Drain and discard marinade from shrimp. Wrap a snow pea around each shrimp; secure with a toothpick. Chill until serving.

YIELD: ABOUT 3 DOZEN.

Earnestine Jackson, Beaumont, Texas

This variation on marinated shrimp gets a splash of color from the snow peas.

herbed deviled eggs

6 hard-cooked eggs

2 tablespoons minced chives

2 tablespoons plain yogurt

2 tablespoons mayonnaise

1 tablespoon chopped fresh tarragon

1 tablespoon minced fresh parsley

2½ teaspoons prepared mustard

1 teaspoon snipped fresh dill

Salt and pepper to taste

Cut eggs in half lengthwise; remove yolks and set whites aside. In a small bowl, mash yolks with a fork. Stir in the remaining ingredients. Pipe or stuff into egg whites. Refrigerate until serving.

YIELD: 1 DOZEN.

Sue Seymour, Valatie, New York

Wondering what to do with hard-cooked eggs when Easter is past? This version of deviled eggs has a delightful twist—I add a mix of herbs to the filling.

salmon canapes

1 package (8 ounces) reduced-fat cream cheese

1 teaspoon snipped fresh dill *or* ¼ teaspoon dill weed

36 slices cocktail rye bread

12 ounces sliced smoked salmon

1 medium red onion, thinly sliced and separated into rings

Fresh dill sprigs, optional

In a small mixing bowl, combine cream cheese and dill. Spread on rye bread. Top with salmon and red onion. Garnish with dill sprigs if desired.

YIELD: 12 SERVINGS.

Tristin Crenshaw, Tucson, Arizona

My boyfriend's mother gave me the idea for this classy appetizer that I serve for Sunday brunch and special occasions like New Year's Eve. The textures and flavors of the dill, cream cheese and smoked salmon are scrumptious together. Spread on cocktail rye bread, it's sure to be the toast of your buffet!

oriental pork tenderloin

1 cup soy sauce

1/2 cup packed brown sugar

2 tablespoons red wine vinegar

2 teaspoons red food coloring, optional

1 garlic clove, minced

1 teaspoon ground ginger

1 teaspoon salt

1/2 teaspoon pepper

3 pork tenderloins (about 1 pound *each*)

Sesame seeds, toasted

1 In a bowl, combine the first eight ingredients; mix well. Remove 1/2 cup for basting; cover and refrigerate. Pour the remaining marinade into a large resealable plastic bag; add tenderloins. Seal bag and turn to coat; refrigerate overnight.

2 Drain and discard marinade from pork. Place pork on a rack in a shallow roasting pan. Bake, uncovered, at 350° for 55-60 minutes or until a meat thermometer reads 160°, brushing with the reserved marinade every 15 minutes.

3 Sprinkle with sesame seeds. Cool for 30 minutes. Refrigerate for 2 hours or overnight. Cut into thin slices.

YIELD: 8-10 SERVINGS.

Diana Beyer, Graham, Washington

I first made this appetizer on Christmas Eve a few years ago, and it has since become a tradition. Serve the pork slices alone or on small dinner rolls with hot mustard sauce, ketchup or horseradish.

nutty apple wedges

1 medium unpeeled tart apple, cored

1/2 cup peanut butter

1 cup crushed cornflakes

Cut apple into 12 thin wedges. Spread peanut butter on cut sides; roll in the cornflakes.

YIELD: 4-6 SERVINGS.

Beatrice Richard, Posen, Michigan

A crunchy coating turns apples and peanut butter into a finger-licking, after-school snack. Even very young kids will have a blast spreading peanut butter on the apple wedges and rolling them in cornflake crumbs.

tortellini appetizers

4 garlic cloves, peeled

2 tablespoons olive oil, *divided*

1 package (10 ounces) refrigerated spinach tortellini

1 cup mayonnaise

¼ cup grated Parmesan cheese

¼ cup milk

¼ cup prepared pesto

⅛ teaspoon pepper

1 pint grape tomatoes

26 frilled toothpicks

1 Place garlic cloves on a double thickness of heavy-duty foil; drizzle with 1 tablespoon oil. Wrap foil around garlic. Bake at 425° for 20-25 minutes or until tender. Cool for 10-15 minutes.

2 Meanwhile, cook tortellini according to package directions; drain and rinse in cold water. Toss with remaining oil; set aside. In a small bowl, combine the mayonnaise, Parmesan cheese, milk, pesto and pepper. Mash garlic into pesto mixture; stir until combined.

3 Alternately thread tortellini and tomatoes onto toothpicks. Serve with pesto dip. Refrigerate leftovers.

YIELD: ABOUT 2 DOZEN (1½ CUPS DIP).

Cheryl Lama, Royal Oak, Michigan

The festive green and red of this appetizer will make it a welcomed addition to your holiday buffet table. Store-bought pesto keeps the preparation fast. Sometimes I like to heat the garlic in a skillet and use skewers for a different look.

red pepper bruschetta

1 whole garlic bulb

1 teaspoon plus 2 tablespoons olive oil, *divided*

2 medium sweet red peppers, halved and seeded

3 tablespoons minced fresh parsley

2 tablespoons minced fresh basil *or* 2 teaspoons dried basil

1 tablespoon lemon juice

½ teaspoon salt

¼ teaspoon pepper

1 French bread baguette (about 12 ounces)

1 Remove papery outer skin from garlic bulb (do not peel or separate cloves). Brush with 1 teaspoon oil. Wrap in heavy-duty foil. Bake at 425° for 30-35 minutes or until softened. Cool.

2 Broil red peppers 4 in. from the heat until skins blister, about 10 minutes. Immediately place peppers in a bowl; cover with plastic wrap and let stand for 15-20 minutes.

3 Peel off and discard charred skin from peppers and coarsely chop. Cut top off garlic head, leaving root end intact. Squeeze softened garlic from bulb and finely chop.

4 In a bowl, combine the parsley, basil, lemon juice, salt, pepper and remaining oil. Add peppers and garlic; mix well. Cut bread into 16 slices, ½ in. thick; broil until lightly toasted. Top with pepper mixture. Serve immediately.

YIELD: 8 SERVINGS.

Taste of Home Test Kitchen

Roasted red peppers take the place of tomatoes in this twist on traditional bruschetta. If your bakery doesn't offer baguettes, buy regular French bread instead then cut the slices in half to create the crunchy snacks.

asian spring rolls

3 tablespoons lime juice

1 tablespoon hoisin sauce

1 teaspoon sugar

1 teaspoon salt

3 ounces uncooked Asian rice noodles

1 large carrot, grated

1 medium cucumber, peeled, seeded and julienned

1 medium jalapeno pepper, seeded and chopped

1/3 cup chopped dry roasted peanuts

8 spring roll wrappers *or* rice papers (8 inches)

1/2 cup loosely packed fresh cilantro

PEANUT SAUCE:

2 garlic cloves, minced

1/2 to 1 teaspoon crushed red pepper flakes

2 teaspoons vegetable oil

1/4 cup hoisin sauce

1/4 cup creamy peanut butter

2 tablespoons tomato paste

1/2 cup hot water

1 In a small bowl, combine the lime juice, hoisin sauce and sugar; set aside. In a large saucepan, bring 2 qts. water and salt to a boil. Add noodles; cook for 2-3 minutes or until tender. Drain and rinse with cold water. Transfer to a bowl and toss with 2 tablespoons reserved lime juice mixture; set aside. In another bowl, combine carrot, cucumber, jalapeno and peanuts. Toss with remaining lime juice mixture; set aside.

2 Soak the spring roll wrappers in cool water for 5 minutes. Carefully separate and place on a flat surface. Top each with several cilantro leaves. Place 1/4 cup carrot mixture and 1/4 cup noodles down the center of each wrapper to within 1 1/2 in. of ends. Fold both ends over filling; fold one long side over the filling, then carefully roll up tightly. Place seam side down on serving plate. Cover with damp paper towels and refrigerate until serving.

3 In a small saucepan, cook garlic and pepper flakes in oil for 2 minutes. Add the remaining sauce ingredients; cook and stir until combined and thickened. Serve with spring rolls.

YIELD: 8 SPRING ROLLS (1 CUP SAUCE).

EDITOR'S NOTE: When cutting or seeding hot peppers, use rubber or plastic gloves to protect your hands. Avoid touching your face.

Nirvana Harris, Mundelein, Illinois

The peanut dipping sauce is slightly spicy but really complements these traditional vegetable-filled spring rolls.

stuffed banana peppers

2 packages (8 ounces *each*) cream cheese, softened

1 envelope ranch salad dressing mix

1 cup (4 ounces) finely shredded cheddar cheese

5 bacon strips, cooked and crumbled

8 mild banana peppers (about 6-inches long), halved lengthwise and seeded

In a small mixing bowl, combine the cream cheese, salad dressing mix, cheese and bacon until blended. Pipe or stuff into pepper halves. Cover and refrigerate until serving. Cut into 1¼-in. pieces.

YIELD: 8-10 SERVINGS.

EDITOR'S NOTE: When cutting or seeding banana peppers, use rubber or plastic gloves to protect your hands. Avoid touching your face.

Cathy Kidd, Medora, Indiana

I received this recipe from a customer while working at my sister's produce market.

The peppers can be made a day in advance, making them great for get-togethers.

pickled eggs and beets

1 can (14½ ounces) sliced beets

½ cup sugar

¼ cup white vinegar

½ cinnamon stick

6 whole cloves, optional

8 hard-cooked eggs, shelled

1 Drain beets, reserving juice. Add enough water to juice to measure ¾ cup; place in saucepan. Add the sugar, vinegar, cinnamon stick and cloves if desired; bring to a boil. Remove from the heat.

2 Place eggs in a bowl; top with beets. Pour liquid over all. Cover and refrigerate for 4 hours or overnight. Remove the cinnamon stick and cloves before serving.

YIELD: 8 SERVINGS.

Ellen Benninger, Stoneboro, Pennsylvania

This is a regional specialty. I like this particular recipe because the eggs are not too puckery, and it's so easy to prepare.

chicken ham pinwheels

4 boneless skinless chicken breast halves

1/8 teaspoon plus 1/2 teaspoon dried basil, *divided*

1/8 teaspoon salt

1/8 teaspoon garlic salt

1/8 teaspoon pepper

4 thin sliced deli ham

2 teaspoons lemon juice

Paprika

1/2 cup mayonnaise

1 teaspoon grated orange peel

1 teaspoon orange juice

1 Flatten chicken to 1/4-in. thickness. Combine 1/8 teaspoon basil, salt, garlic salt and pepper; sprinkle over chicken. Top each with a ham slice.

2 Roll up jelly-roll style; place seam side down in a greased 11-in. x 7-in. x 2-in. baking dish. Drizzle with lemon juice and sprinkle with paprika. Bake, uncovered, at 350° for 30 minutes or until chicken juices run clear. Cover and refrigerate.

3 Meanwhile, in a bowl, combine the mayonnaise, orange peel, orange juice and remaining basil. Cover and refrigerate until serving. Cut chicken rolls into 1/2-in. slices. Serve with orange spread.

YIELD: 24 SERVINGS.

Laura Mahaffey, Annapolis, Maryland

These pretty pinwheels have been a part of our annual Christmas Eve appetizer buffet for many years. I love them because they can be made a day in advance and taste great alone or served with crackers.

asparagus beef roll-ups

1½ cups water

36 fresh asparagus spears, trimmed

1 carton (8 ounces) spreadable chive and onion cream cheese

3 to 5 tablespoons prepared horseradish

2 packages (5 ounces *each*) thinly sliced roast beef

1 In a large skillet, bring water to a boil. Add asparagus; cover and boil for 2-3 minutes or until crisp-tender. Drain and immediately place asparagus in ice water. Drain and pat dry.

2 In a small mixing bowl, combine cream cheese and horseradish. Pat beef slices dry with paper towels. Spread each slice with a thin layer of cream cheese mixture; top with an asparagus spear. Roll up tightly. Refrigerate until serving.

YIELD: 3 DOZEN.

Kris Krueger, Plano, Texas

I create these easy and elegant appetizers with asparagus spears, roast beef slices and a cream cheese-horseradish spread. I make them for all of my parties and have received many recipe requests. They're a snap to assemble.

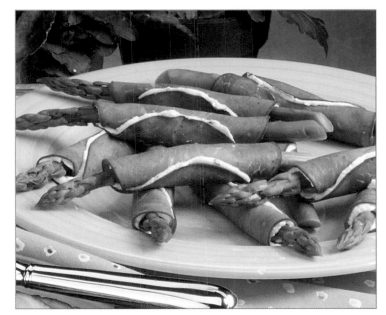

cream-filled strawberries

18 large fresh strawberries

1 cup cold fat-free milk

1 package (1 ounce) sugar-free instant vanilla pudding mix

2 cups reduced-fat whipped topping

¼ teaspoon almond extract

1 Remove stems from strawberries; cut a deep X in the top of each berry. Spread berries apart.

2 In a bowl, whisk milk and pudding mix for 2 minutes. Fold in whipped topping and almond extract. Pipe or spoon about 5 teaspoons into each berry. Chill until serving.

YIELD: 18 STRAWBERRIES.

Karin Poroslay, Wesley Chapel, Florida

These plump berries filled with a creamy pudding mixture are so elegant-looking and luscious-tasting that they're perfect for parties or holiday gatherings.

cucumber canapes

1 cup mayonnaise

1 package (3 ounces) cream cheese, softened

1 tablespoon grated onion

1 tablespoon minced chives

1/2 teaspoon cider vinegar

1/2 teaspoon Worcestershire sauce

1 garlic clove, minced

1/4 teaspoon paprika

1/8 teaspoon curry powder

1/8 teaspoon *each* dried oregano, thyme, basil, parsley flakes and dill weed

1 loaf (1 pound) white *or* rye bread

2 medium cucumbers, scored and thinly sliced

Diced pimientos and additional dill weed

1 In a blender or food processor, combine the mayonnaise, cream cheese, onion, chives, vinegar, Worcestershire sauce and seasonings. Cover and process until blended. Cover and refrigerate for 24 hours.

2 Using a 2½-in. biscuit cutter, cut out circles from bread slices. Spread mayonnaise mixture over bread; top with cucumber slices. Garnish with pimientos and dill.

YIELD: 2 DOZEN.

Nadine Whittaker, South Plymouth, Massachusetts
I always get requests for the recipe whenever I serve these delicate finger sandwiches with a creamy herb spread and festive red and green garnishes.

shrimp salad on endive

1/3 cup mayonnaise

1/2 teaspoon lemon juice

1/4 teaspoon dill weed

1/4 teaspoon seafood seasoning

1/8 teaspoon salt

1/8 teaspoon pepper

1/2 pound cooked shrimp, chopped

1 green onion, sliced

2 tablespoons chopped celery

1 tablespoon diced pimientos

2 heads Belgian endive, separated into leaves

In a small bowl, combine the first six ingredients. Stir in the shrimp, onion, celery and pimientos. Spoon 1 tablespoonful onto each endive leaf; arrange on a platter. Refrigerate until serving.

YIELD: ABOUT 1 1/2 DOZEN.

Taste of Home Test Kitchen

This simple-to-prepare shrimp salad is served on endive leaves for a from-the-sea version of lettuce wraps.

cucumber ham roll-ups

- 1 medium cucumber
- 1 package (8 ounces) cream cheese, softened
- 2 tablespoons prepared mustard
- 1 teaspoon dill weed
- 8 thin rectangular slices deli ham

1 Peel cucumber; cut in half lengthwise. Scoop out seeds with a spoon. Cut each half lengthwise into four strips; set aside.

2 In a small mixing bowl, combine the cream cheese, mustard and dill. Spread about 2 tablespoons over each ham slice. Place a cucumber strip on the wide end; roll up tightly jelly-roll style. Cut off any of the cucumber that extends beyond ham slice. Wrap tightly in plastic wrap and refrigerate for at least 2 hours. Cut into ¾-in. slices.

YIELD: ABOUT 4 DOZEN.

Debbie Smith, Urbana, Ohio
I came across this recipe looking for a new dish to take to a card party. Everyone loves these refreshing roll-ups—even the kids!

guacamole-stuffed eggs

- 6 hard-cooked eggs
- ¼ cup guacamole dip
- 1 teaspoon lime juice
- 1 tablespoon minced fresh cilantro
- ¼ teaspoon salt, optional

Paprika, optional

Cut eggs in half lengthwise; remove yolks and set whites aside. In a small bowl, mash yolks with a fork. Stir in the guacamole, lime juice, cilantro and salt if desired. Pipe or stuff into egg whites. Refrigerate until serving. Sprinkle with paprika if desired. Refrigerate until serving.

YIELD: 1 DOZEN.

Phy Bresse, Lumberton, North Carolina
Looking for a quick and easy way to wish guests "Feliz Navidad?" Try my flavorful south-of-the-border variation on deviled eggs. Guests say they're heavenly.

sweet-sour deviled eggs

12 hard-cooked eggs

1/3 cup plus 1 tablespoon mayonnaise

5 teaspoons sugar

5 teaspoons cider vinegar

1 teaspoon prepared mustard

1/2 teaspoon salt

1/4 teaspoon pepper

Paprika and minced fresh parsley

Slice eggs in half lengthwise; remove yolks and set whites aside. In a small bowl, mash yolks with a fork. Add the mayonnaise, sugar, vinegar, mustard, salt and pepper. Pipe or stuff into egg whites. Garnish with paprika and parsley. Refrigerate until serving.

YIELD: 2 DOZEN.

Claudia Millhouse, Myersville, Maryland

Folks will be sweet on these appetizers when they try them! My family doesn't like traditional deviled eggs, but they gobble this sweet-sour version right up.

antipasto kabobs

- 1 package (9 ounces) refrigerated cheese tortellini
- 40 pimiento-stuffed olives
- 40 large pitted ripe olives
- ¾ cup Italian salad dressing
- 40 thin slices pepperoni
- 20 thin slices hard salami, halved

1 Cook tortellini according to package directions; drain and rinse in cold water.

2 In a resealable plastic bag, combine the tortellini, olives and salad dressing. Seal and refrigerate for 4 hours or overnight.

3 Drain and discard dressing. For each appetizer, thread a stuffed olive, folded pepperoni slice, tortellini, folded salami piece and ripe olive on a toothpick or short skewer.

YIELD: 40 APPETIZERS.

Denise Hazen, Cincinnati, Ohio
My husband and I met at a cooking class, and we have loved creating menus and entertaining ever since. These do-ahead appetizers are always a hit.

pork pinwheels

GARLIC MAYONNAISE:
1 large whole garlic bulb

2 teaspoons olive oil

½ cup mayonnaise

1 to 3 teaspoons milk, optional

STUFFING:
3 medium leeks (white portion only), thinly sliced

4 tablespoons olive oil, *divided*

1 cup minced fresh parsley

¼ cup grated Parmesan cheese

1 tablespoon minced fresh thyme *or* 1 teaspoon dried thyme

¼ teaspoon salt

¼ teaspoon pepper

¼ cup chopped walnuts

2 pork tenderloins (¾ pound *each*)

1 Remove the papery outer skin from garlic (do not peel or separate cloves). Cut top off garlic bulb. Brush with oil. Wrap bulb in heavy-duty foil. Bake at 425° for 30-35 minutes or until softened. Cool for 10-15 minutes. Squeeze softened garlic into a small bowl; mash until smooth. Stir in mayonnaise and milk if needed to achieve a creamy consistency. Cover and refrigerate for at least 3 hours.

2 In a large skillet, saute leeks in 1 tablespoon oil until tender; remove from the heat. In a blender or food processor, combine the parsley, Parmesan cheese, thyme, salt and pepper. While processing, gradually add the remaining oil until creamy. Add walnuts and leek mixture; coarsely chop. Set aside.

3 Make a lengthwise slit in each tenderloin to within ½ in. of the opposite side. Open tenderloins so they lie flat; cover with plastic wrap. Flatten to ¾-in. thickness; remove plastic wrap. Spread leek mixture to within 1 in. of edges. Roll up from a long side; tie with kitchen string to secure. Place tenderloins seam down on a rack in a shallow roasting pan. Bake, uncovered, at 325° for 45-55 minutes or until a meat thermometer reads 160°. Let stand for 15 minutes. Cover and refrigerate. Discard string; cut pork into ½-in. slices. Serve with garlic mayonnaise.

YIELD: ABOUT 2½ DOZEN.

Mary Lou Wayman, Salt Lake City, Utah

A flavorful filling peeks out from the swirled slices of pork.

This appetizer is enhanced with garlic mayonnaise.

crispy cheese twists

6 tablespoons butter, softened

1 garlic clove, minced

1/8 teaspoon pepper

1 cup (4 ounces) shredded cheddar cheese

2 tablespoons milk

1 tablespoon minced fresh parsley

1 tablespoon snipped fresh dill *or* 1 teaspoon dill weed

1 cup all-purpose flour

1 In a mixing bowl, combine the butter, garlic and pepper; beat until light and fluffy. Stir in cheese, milk, parsley and dill. Gradually add flour, mixing thoroughly.

2 Divide dough into 20 pieces. Roll each piece into a 10-in. log; cut each in half and twist together. Place 1 in. apart on an ungreased baking sheet. Bake at 375° for 10-12 minutes or until golden brown. Remove to wire racks to cool.

YIELD: 20 TWISTS.

Mary Maxeiner, Lakewood, Colorado

My grown son enjoys these cheese twists so much that I'll often bake an extra batch for his stocking stuffer. They make a great anytime snack.

white bean bruschetta

1 cup canned great northern beans, rinsed and drained

3 plum tomatoes, seeded and chopped

1/4 cup chopped pitted Greek olives

6 tablespoons olive oil, *divided*

1/4 cup fresh basil leaves, cut into strips

1 tablespoon minced garlic

Salt and pepper to taste

1 French bread baguette, cut into 1/3-inch-thick slices

1 package (5.3 ounces) goat cheese

In a medium bowl, combine the beans, tomatoes, olives, 4 tablespoons oil, basil, garlic, salt and pepper. Place bread slices on an ungreased baking sheet. Brush with remaining oil. Broil 3-4 in. from the heat until golden, about 1 minute. Spread with cheese; top with bean mixture. Serve immediately.

YIELD: ABOUT 20 SERVINGS.

Kristin Arnett, Elkhorn, Wisconsin

This fabulous bruschetta has a Tuscan flavor. I've made it many times to serve when entertaining guests because it's quick & easy.

savory cheese cutouts

J.R. Smosna, Warren, Pennsylvania

This recipe is always a success because the dough is easy to work with and cuts well. The appetizer can be made year-round using cookie cutter shapes to suit the season.

2 cups all-purpose flour

1 cup (4 ounces) shredded Swiss cheese

1 teaspoon sugar

1 teaspoon salt

1/2 teaspoon ground mustard

1/8 to 1/4 teaspoon cayenne pepper

1/2 cup plus 2 tablespoons cold butter

9 tablespoons dry white wine *or* chicken broth

1 egg, lightly beaten

Sesame seeds *and/or* poppy seeds

1 In a bowl, combine the first six ingredients; cut in butter until the mixture resembles coarse crumbs. Gradually add wine or broth, tossing with a fork until dough forms a ball.

2 On a lightly floured surface, roll out dough to 1/8-in. thickness. Cut with floured 2-in. cookie cutters. Place 1 in. apart on ungreased baking sheets.

3 Brush tops with egg; sprinkle with sesame and/or poppy seeds. Bake at 400° for 10-12 minutes or until lightly browned. Remove to wire racks to cool.

YIELD: 6 DOZEN.

fruit 'n' cheese kabobs

1 block (1 pound) Colby-Monterey Jack cheese

1 block (1 pound) cheddar cheese

1 block (1 pound) baby Swiss cheese

1 fresh pineapple, peeled, cored and cut into 2-inch chunks

1 to 2 pounds seedless green *or* red grapes

3 pints strawberries

Cut cheese into chunks or slices. If desired, cut into shapes with small cutters. Alternately thread cheese and fruit onto wooden skewers. Serve immediately.

YIELD: ABOUT 3 DOZEN.

Taste of Home Test Kitchen

This simple, nutritious snack is a snap to put together, much to the delight of busy cooks!

shrimp lover squares

1 tube (8 ounces) refrigerated crescent rolls

1 package (8 ounces) cream cheese, softened

¼ cup sour cream

½ teaspoon dill weed

⅛ teaspoon salt

½ cup seafood sauce

24 cooked medium shrimp, peeled and deveined

½ cup chopped green pepper

⅓ cup chopped onion

1 cup (4 ounces) shredded Monterey Jack cheese

1 In a greased 13-in. x 9-in. x 2-in. baking dish, unroll crescent dough into one long rectangle; seal seams and perforations. Bake at 375° for 10-12 minutes or until golden brown. Cool completely on a wire rack.

2 In a small mixing bowl, beat the cream cheese, sour cream, dill and salt until smooth. Spread over crust. Top with seafood sauce, shrimp, green pepper, onion and cheese. Cover and refrigerate for 1 hour. Cut into squares.

YIELD: 2 DOZEN.

Ardyce Piehl, Poynette, Wisconsin

These delicious shrimp squares are part of an appetizer buffet I prepare for family every Christmas. During the holidays, we enjoy having a variety of appetizers as a meal while playing a board game or watching a movie together.

marinated mushrooms and cheese

½ cup sun-dried tomatoes (not packed in oil), julienned

1 cup boiling water

½ cup olive oil

½ cup white wine vinegar

2 garlic cloves, minced

½ teaspoon salt

½ pound sliced fresh mushrooms

8 ounces Monterey Jack cheese, cubed

In a small bowl, combine the tomatoes and water. Let stand for 5 minutes; drain. In a large resealable plastic bag, combine the oil, vinegar, garlic and salt; add the tomatoes, mushrooms and cheese. Seal bag and toss to coat. Refrigerate for at least 4 hours before serving. Drain and discard marinade.

YIELD: 12-14 SERVINGS.

Kim Marie Van Rheenen, Mendota, Illinois

I like to serve these savory mushrooms alongside sliced baguettes and crackers. They're colorful and so versatile. You might like to vary the cheese or add olives, artichokes or a little basil.

garlic tomato bruschetta

¼ cup olive oil

3 tablespoons chopped fresh basil

3 to 4 garlic cloves, minced

½ teaspoon salt

¼ teaspoon pepper

4 medium tomatoes, diced

2 tablespoons grated Parmesan cheese

1 loaf (1 pound) unsliced French bread

1 In a bowl, combine the oil, basil, garlic, salt and pepper. Add tomatoes and toss gently. Sprinkle with cheese. Refrigerate for at least 1 hour.

2 Bring to room temperature before serving. Cut bread into 24 slices; toast under broiler until lightly browned Top with tomato mixture. Serve immediately.

YIELD: 12 SERVINGS.

Jean Franzoni, Rutland, Vermont

Bruschetta is a popular snack because it is made with fresh and flavorful ingredients and is so tasty.

cucumber whimsies

2 cans (6 ounces *each*) crabmeat, drained, flaked and cartilage removed

¼ cup mayonnaise

1 small tomato, chopped

2 tablespoons snipped fresh dill

1 green onion, chopped

1 teaspoon grated lemon peel

⅛ teaspoon cayenne pepper

Dash salt

3 medium cucumbers, cut into ¼-inch slices

Lemon-pepper seasoning

Dill sprigs

1 In a large bowl, combine the first eight ingredients. Cover and chill for 1 hour.

2 Sprinkle the cucumber slices with lemon-pepper. Top each with about 1½ teaspoons crab mixture; garnish with a dill sprig. Refrigerate until serving.

YIELD: 5 DOZEN.

Cheryl Stevens, Carrollton, Texas

During the heat of summer, it's nice to offer lighter fare. These cold snacks are a great addition to a picnic buffet.

smoked salmon new potatoes

36 small red potatoes (about 1½ pounds)

1 package (8 ounces) reduced-fat cream cheese, cubed

2 packages (3 ounces *each*) smoked cooked salmon

2 tablespoons chopped green onion

2 teaspoons dill weed

2 teaspoons lemon juice

⅛ teaspoon salt

⅛ teaspoon pepper

Fresh dill sprigs

1 Place the potatoes in a large saucepan and cover with water. Bring to a boil. Reduce heat; simmer, uncovered, for 20-22 minutes or until tender.

2 Meanwhile, in a food processor or blender, combine the cream cheese, salmon, onion, dill, lemon juice, salt and pepper. Cover and process until smooth; set aside.

3 Drain potatoes and immediately place in ice water. Drain and pat dry with paper towels. Cut a thin slice off the bottom of each potato to allow it to sit flat. With a melon baller, scoop out a small amount of potato (discard or save for another use). Pipe or spoon salmon mixture into potatoes. Garnish with dill sprigs.

YIELD: 3 DOZEN.

Taste of Home Test Kitchen

This recipe proves that delicious party food and healthy eating are compatible. Plus, you're bound to get rave reviews when guests uncover these baby stuffed potatoes. If you're in a hurry, you can serve the cream cheese mixture as a spread with whole wheat crackers.

tangy mozzarella bites

¼ cup olive oil

1 to 2 teaspoons balsamic vinegar

1 garlic clove, minced

1 teaspoon dried basil

1 teaspoon coarsely ground pepper

1 pound mozzarella cheese, cut into
  ½-inch cubes

In a bowl, combine the oil, vinegar, garlic, basil and pepper. Add cheese; toss to coat. Cover and refrigerate for at least 1 hour.

YIELD: ABOUT 3 CUPS.

Julie Wasem, Aurora, Nebraska

I adapted this recipe from one I found years ago, substituting ingredients most people have on hand. I like to serve it with crackers or small bread slices.

crunchy munchies

220

219

Let your guests nibble and nosh on crisp, flavorful treats of popcorn, snack mixes and seasoned nuts while you entertain. Sweet or savory—there's a lot to choose from, such as Deluxe Caramel Corn (p. 227), Harvest Snack Mix (p. 220) and Cinnamon 'n' Spice Pecans (p. 219).

Set out these easy-to-make snacks in bowls with a scoop or serve them up in popcorn bags, large paper cups or small brown paper lunch bags. Kids and adults alike will love them!

cajun party mix

6 cups miniature fish-shaped crackers

6 cups pretzel sticks

3 cups Rice Chex

3 cups Corn Chex

1 can (11½ ounces) mixed nuts

1 cup butter, melted

1 teaspoon garlic powder

½ to 1 teaspoon celery salt

½ teaspoon cayenne pepper

⅛ teaspoon hot pepper sauce

1 In a large roasting pan, combine the first five ingredients. Combine the butter, garlic powder, celery salt, cayenne and hot pepper sauce; pour over cereal mixture and stir to coat.

2 Bake, uncovered, at 250° for 35-40 minutes, stirring every 15 minutes. Cool completely. Store in airtight containers.

YIELD: ABOUT 5 QUARTS.

Twila Burkholder, Middleburg, Pennsylvania

I pack this mix in Christmas tins to give to friends and family. They can't seem to get enough—and it's so easy!

cinnamon 'n' spice pecans

⅓ cup butter, melted

2 teaspoons ground cinnamon

¾ teaspoon salt

½ teaspoon cayenne pepper

1 pound pecan halves

In a bowl, combine the butter, cinnamon, salt and cayenne. Stir in pecans until evenly coated. Transfer to an ungreased 15-in. x 10-in. x 1-in. baking pan. Bake at 350° for 15-18 minutes or until pecans are toasted, stirring every 5 minutes.

YIELD: 4 CUPS.

Terry Maly, Olathe, Kansas

Originally, these crunchy nuts were used to top a salad, but I adjusted the recipe so they could stand on their own as a snack. Cayenne pepper gives them a little kick, making the nuts a fun party starter or hostess gift.

harvest snack mix

Marlene Harguth, Maynard, Minnesota

Candy corn makes this a natural snack for fall gatherings. The sweet and salty flavors are irresistible to many.

2 cups pretzel sticks

1 cup mixed nuts

½ cup sunflower kernels

6 tablespoons butter, melted

½ teaspoon ground cinnamon

⅛ teaspoon ground cloves

8 cups popped popcorn

1 cup candy corn

1 cup chocolate bridge mix

1 In a large bowl, combine the pretzels, nuts and sunflower kernels. Combine the butter, cinnamon and cloves. Drizzle a third of butter mixture over pretzel mixture; toss to coat. Transfer to a greased 15-in. x 10-in. x 1-in. baking pan. Bake at 300° for 15 minutes.

2 Place popcorn in a large bowl; drizzle with remaining butter mixture and toss to coat. Stir into pretzel mixture. Bake 15 minutes longer or until heated through. Cool; transfer to a large bowl. Add candy corn and bridge mix; toss to combine.

YIELD: 3 QUARTS.

peanut butter chocolate pretzels

2 cups (12 ounces) semisweet
  chocolate chips

4 teaspoons vegetable oil, *divided*

35 to 40 large thin pretzel twists

½ cup peanut butter chips

1 In a microwave or heavy saucepan, melt chocolate chips and 3 teaspoons oil until smooth. Dip pretzels; shake off excess. Place on waxed paper-lined baking sheets to set.

2 Melt the peanut butter chips and remaining oil; transfer to a small resealable bag. Cut a small hole in the corner of bag; drizzle over half of the pretzels. Let dry. Store in an airtight container.

YIELD: ABOUT 3 DOZEN.

Marcia Porch, Winter Park, Florida

The treats are easy for any age to make but pretty enough to share with friends. You can add color sprinkles to customize them for any holiday or occasion.

honey snack mix

1 package (10 ounces) honey-flavored bear-shaped graham crackers (about 4 cups)

3 cups Honeycomb cereal

1½ cups Reese's Pieces

1 cup chocolate-covered raisins

In a large bowl, combine all the ingredients. Store in an airtight container.

YIELD: 9 CUPS.

Taste of Home Test Kitchen

Little cubs can't resist gobbling up the crackers, cereal, raisins and candy in this sweet snack mix.

---

italian nut medley

2 tablespoons butter

4 cups mixed nuts

1 tablespoon soy sauce

1 envelope Italian salad dressing mix

In a skillet, melt the butter over medium heat. Add nuts; cook and stir constantly for 2 minutes. Stir in soy sauce. Sprinkle with salad dressing mix; stir to coat. Immediately transfer to a greased baking pan and spread in a single layer. Cool. Store in an airtight container.

YIELD: 4 CUPS.

Karen Riordan, Fern Creek, Kentucky

Italian salad dressing mix is the easy secret ingredient—it adds just the right zip to plain mixed nuts.

---

white chocolate party mix

16 cups popped popcorn

3 cups Frosted Cheerios

1½ cups pecan halves

1 package (14 ounces) milk chocolate M&M's

1 package (10 ounces) fat-free pretzel sticks

1 package English toffee bits (10 ounces) *or* almond brickle bits (7½ ounces)

2 packages (10 to 12 ounces *each*) vanilla *or* white chips

2 tablespoons vegetable oil

In a large bowl, combine the first six ingredients. In a microwave or heavy saucepan, melt chips and oil; stir until smooth. Pour over popcorn mixture and toss to coat. Immediately spread onto two baking sheets; let stand until dry, about 2 hours. Store in an airtight container.

YIELD: 9½ QUARTS.

Rose Wentzel, St. Louis, Missouri

I get rave reviews every time I prepare this tasty, crispy combination of cereal, popcorn, pretzels, nuts and candies. Coated in white chocolate, this mix is great for meetings, parties and gift giving.

cinnamon granola

2 cups old-fashioned oats

¾ cup whole unsalted nuts

⅔ cup flaked coconut

½ cup sunflower kernels

⅓ cup sesame seeds

⅓ cup toasted wheat germ

¼ cup oat bran

2 tablespoons cornmeal

2 tablespoons whole wheat flour

1 tablespoon ground cinnamon

½ cup honey

2 tablespoons vegetable oil

2 tablespoons vanilla extract

¼ teaspoon salt

1 cup golden raisins

1 In a large bowl, combine the first 10 ingredients; mix well. In a saucepan, heat honey and oil over medium heat for 4-5 minutes. Remove from the heat; stir in vanilla and salt. Pour over oat mixture and toss to coat.

2 Transfer to a greased 15-in. x 10-in. x 1-in. baking pan. Bake at 275° for 45-50 minutes or until golden brown, stirring every 15 minutes. Cool, stirring occasionally. Stir in raisins. Store in an airtight container.

YIELD: 7 CUPS.

Linda Agresta, Colorado Springs, Colorado

Although it's meant for breakfast, my family eats this crunchy cereal by the handful all day long.

seasoned snack mix

3 cups Rice Chex

3 cups Corn Chex

3 cups Cheerios

3 cups pretzels

2 teaspoons Worcestershire sauce

2 teaspoons butter-flavored sprinkles

½ teaspoon garlic powder

½ teaspoon seasoned salt

½ teaspoon onion powder

1 In a 15-in. x 10-in. x 1-in. baking pan, combine cereals and pretzels. Lightly coat with nonstick cooking spray; drizzle with Worcestershire sauce. Combine the remaining ingredients and sprinkle over cereal mixture.

2 Bake at 200° for 1½ hours, stirring every 30 minutes. Cool completely. Store in an airtight container.

YIELD: 3 QUARTS.

Flo Burtnett, Gage, Oklahoma

You'll never miss the oil or nuts in this crispy, deliciously seasoned party mix. I keep some on hand for whenever the munchies strike.

deluxe caramel corn

- 4 quarts plain popped popcorn
- 5 cups mini pretzel twists
- 2 cups packed brown sugar
- 1 cup butter
- 1/2 cup dark corn syrup
- 1/2 teaspoon salt
- 1/2 teaspoon baking soda
- 1 cup salted peanuts
- 2 cups nonchocolate candy (Skittles, gumdrops, etc.)

1 Place popcorn and pretzels in a large bowl; set aside. In a large heavy saucepan, combine the brown sugar, butter, corn syrup and salt; cook over medium heat, stirring occasionally, until mixture comes to a rolling boil. Cook and stir until candy thermometer reads 238° (soft-ball stage). Remove from the heat; stir in baking soda. Quickly pour over popcorn and mix thoroughly; stir in peanuts.

2 Turn into two greased 13-in. x 9-in. x 2-in. baking pans. Bake at 200° for 20 minutes; stir. Bake 25 minutes longer. Remove from the oven; add candy and mix well. Remove from pans and place on waxed paper to cool. Break into clusters. Store in airtight containers or plastic bags.

YIELD: 6 1/2 QUARTS.

EDITOR'S NOTE: You should test your candy thermometer each time you use it. To do this, simply place the thermometer in a saucepan of boiling water and wait for several minutes. If the thermometer reads 212° in boiling water, it is accurate. If it rises above 212° or does not reach 212°, add or subtract the difference to the temperature called for in the recipe you're making.

Lisa Claas, Watertown, Wisconsin
A batch of this colorful crunchy mix is perfect for gift giving or serving at a holiday party.

spicy nuts

Laurene Nickel, Niagara on the Lake, Ontario

Cayenne pepper gives nuts a bit of a kick and a nice flavor contrast to the coriander, cinnamon and cloves. My son-in-law can't get enough of these crunchy treats.

1 tablespoon vegetable oil

2 cups cashews *or* whole unblanched almonds

½ to 1 teaspoon cayenne pepper

½ teaspoon ground coriander

¼ teaspoon salt

Dash *each* ground cinnamon and cloves

1 In a heavy skillet, heat oil over medium heat; add nuts. Cook and stir for 3-5 minutes or until lightly browned; drain. Add the seasonings; stir to coat. Cool completely.

2 To serve warm, place in a baking pan. Heat at 300° for 5 minutes.

YIELD: 2 CUPS.

snackin' granola

2²/₃ cups flaked coconut

1 cup quick-cooking oats

¼ cup packed brown sugar

¼ cup raisins *or* chopped pitted dried plums

¼ cup chopped dried apricots

2 tablespoons sesame seeds

¼ cup vegetable oil

¼ cup honey

¼ cup semisweet chocolate chips *or* M&M's

1 In a large metal bowl, combine the first six ingredients. In a small saucepan, bring the oil and honey to just a boil. Immediately remove from the heat; pour over coconut mixture, stirring to coat evenly.

2 Spread in an ungreased 13-in. x 9-in. x 2-in. baking pan. Bake at 325° for 25 minutes, stirring several times. Transfer to waxed paper to cool. Sprinkle with chocolate chips or M&M's. Store in an airtight container.

YIELD: 7 CUPS.

Marlene Mohr, Cincinnati, Ohio

Granola's a popular treat with children these days—and this one couldn't be more convenient to prepare. I flavor it with lots of tasty good-for-you ingredients. It's perfect to send in bag lunches or to serve after school. I've also used it as an in-the-car treat when we take family vacations.

sweet minglers

1 cup (6 ounces) semisweet chocolate chips

¼ cup creamy peanut butter

6 cups Corn or Rice Chex

1 cup confectioners' sugar

1 In a large microwave-safe bowl, melt chocolate chips on high for 1 minute. Stir; microwave 30 seconds longer or until the chips are melted. Stir in peanut butter. Gently stir in cereal until well coated; set aside.

2 Place confectioners' sugar in a 2-gallon plastic storage bag. Add cereal mixture and shake until well coated. Store in an airtight container in the refrigerator.

YIELD: ABOUT 6 CUPS.

Mary Obeilin, Selinsgrove, Pennsylvania

This snack mix is perfect for a late-night treat or a pick-me-up anytime of the day. I sometimes take a batch to work, and it's always eaten up quickly. It's a slightly different cereal snack because of the chocolate and peanut butter.

critter crunch

¼ cup butter

3 tablespoons brown sugar

1 teaspoon ground cinnamon

1½ cups Crispix

1½ cups Cherrios

1½ cups animal crackers

1½ cups honey-flavored bear-shaped graham crackers

1 cup bite-size Shredded Wheat

1 cup miniature pretzels

1 In a saucepan or microwave-safe bowl, heat the butter, brown sugar and cinnamon until butter is melted; mix well. In a large bowl, combine the remaining ingredients. Add butter mixture and toss to coat.

2 Place in a greased 15-in. x 10-in. x 1-in. baking pan. Bake, uncovered, at 300° for 30 minutes, stirring every 10 minutes. Store in an airtight container.

YIELD: ABOUT 8 CUPS.

Wilma Miller, Port Angeles, Washington

Young kids will enjoy this fun snack that features a variety of wild animals.

cheese ball snack mix

1½ cups salted cashews

1 cup crisp cheese balls snacks

1 cup Corn Chex

1 cup Rice Chex

1 cup miniature pretzels

1 cup chow mein noodles

½ cup butter, melted

1 tablespoon soy sauce

1 teaspoon Worcestershire sauce

½ teaspoon seasoned salt

¼ teaspoon chili powder

¼ teaspoon hot pepper sauce

1 In a bowl, combine the cashews, cheese balls, cereals, pretzels and chow mein noodles. In another bowl, combine all the remaining ingredients. Pour over cereal mixture and toss to coat.

2 Transfer to an ungreased 15-in. x 10-in. x 1-in. baking pan. Bake at 250° for 1 hour, stirring every 15 minutes.

YIELD: ABOUT 6 CUPS.

EDITOR'S NOTE: This recipe was tested with Planter's Cheeze Balls.

Mary Detweiler, West Farmington, Ohio
Folks love the zippy burst of flavor in every bite of this crunchy snack mix.

iced almonds

1/4 cup butter

2 1/2 cups whole unblanched almonds

1 cup sugar

1 teaspoon vanilla extract

1 In a heavy saucepan, melt butter over medium-high heat. Add almonds and sugar. Cook and stir constantly for 7-8 minutes or until syrup is golden brown. Remove from the heat; stir in vanilla.

2 Immediately drop by clusters or separate almonds on a greased baking pan. Cool. Store in an airtight container.

YIELD: 4 CUPS.

Susan Marie Taccone, Erie, Pennsylvania

These sweet almonds make a special snack as s, used to dress up a salad or to garnish on a dessert.

pretzel snackers

2 packages (16 ounces *each*) sourdough pretzel nuggets

1 envelope ranch salad dressing mix

1 1/2 teaspoons dried oregano

1 teaspoon lemon-pepper seasoning

1 teaspoon dill weed

1/2 teaspoon garlic powder

1/2 teaspoon onion powder

1/4 cup olive oil

1 Place pretzels in a large bowl. In a small bowl, combine the dressing mix, oregano, lemon-pepper, dill weed, garlic powder and onion powder. Sprinkle over pretzels; toss gently to combine. Drizzle with oil; toss until well coated.

2 Spread in a 15-in. x 10-in. x 1-in. baking pan coated with nonstick cooking spray. Bake, uncovered, at 350° for 10 minutes. Stir and bake 5 minutes longer. Cool completely. Store in airtight containers.

YIELD: 10 CUPS.

Elissa Armbruster, Medford, New Jersey

I first served this snack when my husband's aunt came to visit and she asked for the recipe. She has since reported that all her friends enjoy it as much as we do! The recipe can easily be doubled or tripled.

cracker snack mix

12 cups original flavor Bugles

6 cups miniature pretzels

1 package (11 ounces) miniature butter-flavored crackers

1 package (10 ounces) Wheat Thins

1 package (9¼ ounces) Cheese Nips

1 package (7½ ounces) nacho cheese Bugles

1 package (6 ounces) miniature Parmesan fish-shaped crackers

1 cup mixed nuts *or* peanuts

1 bottle (10 *or* 12 ounces) butter-flavored popcorn oil

2 envelopes ranch salad dressing mix

1 In a very large bowl, combine the first eight ingredients. In a small bowl, combine oil and salad dressing mix. Pour over cracker mixture; toss to coat evenly.

2 Transfer to four ungreased 15-in. x 10-in. x 1-in. baking pans. Bake at 250° for 45 minutes, stirring every 15 minutes. Cool completely, stirring several times.

YIELD: ABOUT 8 QUARTS.

Sharon Nichols, Brookings, South Dakota
Family and friends will munch this fun mix of crackers, nuts and ranch dressing by the handfuls! Everyone is sure to find something they like. If not, substitute other snack packages to vary the flavors.

chocolaty popcorn

12 cups butter-flavored microwave popcorn

1 package (12 ounces) semisweet chocolate chips

2 teaspoons shortening, *divided*

1 package (10 to 12 ounces) vanilla *or* white chips

2 cups coarsely chopped pecans, toasted

1 Place the popcorn in a greased 15-in. x 10-in. x 1-in. pan; set aside. Place semisweet chocolate chips and 1 teaspoon shortening in a microwave-safe bowl. Microwave, uncovered, at 70% power for 1 minute; stir until smooth. Drizzle over popcorn.

2 Place vanilla chips and remaining shortening in a microwave-safe bowl. Microwave, uncovered, at 70% power for 1 minute; stir until smooth. Drizzle over popcorn; toss gently to coat as much popcorn as possible. Sprinkle with pecans. Chill until firm before breaking into pieces.

YIELD: 16 CUPS.

EDITOR'S NOTE: This recipe was tested in a 1,100-watt microwave.

Diane Halferty, Corpus Christi, Texas
Pack this irresistible snack into wax or plastic bags and tie them shut with curling ribbons for a pretty presentation. You could also prepare a batch or two for a holiday bake sale. I guarantee it'll go quickly!

sweet bites

Satisfy anyone's sweet tooth with one or two mini desserts. Individual sweets are a delectable complement to heartier appetizers. Let guests sample Cheese-Filled Shortbread Tarts (p. 240), French Vanilla Cream Puffs (p. 242), Sugared Raisin Pear Diamonds (p. 238) or one of the other sensational delights included here.

You'll find the make-ahead convenience of these creations a real plus. Before the party, just arrange on serving dishes and place them on the side. Then add them to the buffet halfway through the party.

sugared raisin pear diamonds

2½ cups plus 4½ teaspoons all-purpose flour, *divided*

¼ cup plus 6 tablespoons sugar, *divided*

½ teaspoon salt

¾ cup cold butter

½ teaspoon grated lemon peel

½ cup half-and-half cream

6 cups diced peeled ripe pears (about 7)

6 tablespoons golden raisins

¼ cup lemon juice

⅛ to ¼ teaspoon ground cinnamon

1 egg, lightly beaten

Additional sugar

1 In a bowl, combine 2½ cups flour, ¼ cup sugar and salt. Cut in butter and lemon peel until the mixture resembles coarse crumbs. Gradually add cream, tossing with a fork until dough forms a ball.

2 Divide in half. Roll out one portion of dough onto lightly floured waxed paper or pastry cloth into a 16-in. x 11½-in. rectangle. Transfer to an ungreased 15-in. x 10-in. x 1-in. baking pan.

3 Bake at 350° for 10-15 minutes or until lightly browned. Cool on a wire rack. Increase temperature to 400°.

4 In a bowl, combine the pears, raisins, lemon juice, cinnamon and remaining flour and sugar. Spread over crust. Roll out remaining dough into a 16-in. x 12-in. rectangle; place over filling. Trim and seal edges. Brush top with egg; sprinkle with additional sugar.

5 Bake for 30-34 minutes or until golden brown. Cool on a wire rack. Cut into diamond-shaped bars.

YIELD: ABOUT 2 DOZEN.

Jeanne Allen, Rye, Colorado

With their tender, golden crust and tempting pear and raisin filling, these fabulous bars stand out on any buffet table. Substitute apples for the pears, and you'll still get yummy results!

berry nut tarts

½ cup butter, softened

1 package (3 ounces) cream cheese, softened

1 cup all-purpose flour

FILLING:

1½ cups packed brown sugar

2 tablespoons butter, melted

2 eggs, lightly beaten

2 teaspoons vanilla extract

⅔ cup finely chopped cranberries

⅓ cup chopped pecans

1 In a small mixing bowl, beat the butter and cream cheese; add flour and mix well. Cover and refrigerate for 1 hour or until easy to handle.

2 Cut dough into 12 portions. Press onto the bottom and all the way up the sides of greased muffin cups. In a bowl, combine the brown sugar, butter, eggs and vanilla. Stir in the cranberries and pecans. Spoon into prepared crusts.

3 Bake at 350° for 25-30 minutes or until edges are golden brown. Cool for 5 minutes before removing from pan to a wire rack to cool completely. Store in the refrigerator.

YIELD: ABOUT 1 DOZEN.

Lena Ehlert, Vancouver, British Columbia

Cranberries are a delicious addition to this spin on individual pecan pies. Folks have a hard time eating just one!

cheese-filled shortbread tartlets

1 package (8 ounces) cream cheese, softened

1 cup sweetened condensed milk

1/3 cup lemon juice

1 teaspoon vanilla extract

1 cup butter, softened

1 1/2 cups all-purpose flour

1/2 cup confectioners' sugar

1 tablespoon cornstarch

Fresh raspberries and mint leaves for garnish

1 In a small mixing bowl, beat cream cheese until smooth. Gradually beat in the milk, lemon juice and vanilla. Cover and refrigerate for 8 hours or overnight.

2 In another mixing bowl, beat the butter, flour, confectioners' sugar and cornstarch until smooth. Roll into 1-in. balls. Place in greased miniature muffin cups; press onto the bottom and up the sides. Prick with a fork.

3 Bake at 325° for 20-25 minutes or until golden brown. Immediately run a knife around each tart to loosen. Cool in pans on wire racks.

4 Pipe or spoon 1 tablespoon of the cheese filling into each tart shell. Cover and refrigerate until set. Just before serving, garnish as desired.

YIELD: 3 DOZEN.

Cathy Walerius, Mound, Minnesota
Bite-size treats are a nice addition to a dessert buffet. You can store cooled, baked tart shells in an airtight container at room temperature overnight or in the freezer for a few weeks.

strawberry cookie tarts

½ cup vanilla *or* white chips, melted and slightly cooled

1 package (3 ounces) cream cheese, softened

½ cup whipped topping

¼ cup confectioners' sugar

1 teaspoon lemon juice

½ teaspoon vanilla extract

12 sugar cookies (about 2½ inches)

4 to 5 fresh strawberries, sliced

In a small mixing bowl, beat the melted chips, cream cheese, whipped topping, sugar, lemon juice and vanilla until smooth. Spread about 1 heaping tablespoon onto each cookie. Top with sliced strawberries. Refrigerate until serving.

YIELD: 1 DOZEN.

Taste of Home Test Kitchen

For an even more festive touch on the Fourth of July, top half of the cookies with strawberries or raspberries and the other half with blueberries.

marmalade turnovers

½ cup butter, softened

1 jar (5 ounces) sharp American cheese spread

1 cup all-purpose flour

⅓ cup marmalade

1 In a bowl, combine butter and cheese. Add flour; stir until mixture forms a ball. Cover and refrigerate for 1 hour. On a lightly floured surface, roll dough to ⅛-in. thickness; cut into 2¾-in. circles. Place ½ teaspoon marmalade on each circle. Fold pastry over and seal edges with a fork. Cut slits in top of pastry.

2 Place 2-in. apart on ungreased baking sheets. Bake at 350° for 5-9 minutes or until lightly browned. Remove to wire racks to cool.

YIELD: 2½ DOZEN.

Anna Jean Allen, West Liberty, Kentucky

A church friend prepares these delicate pastries for gatherings, but they're usually gone before she gets the platter to the serving table.

french vanilla cream puffs

1 cup water

½ cup butter

1 cup all-purpose flour

¼ teaspoon salt

4 eggs

FILLING:

1½ cups cold milk

1 package (3.4 ounces) instant French vanilla pudding mix

1 cup whipped topping

1 package (12 ounces) miniature semisweet chocolate chips

Confectioners' sugar

1 In a saucepan, bring water and butter to a boil. Add flour and salt all at once; stir until a smooth ball forms. Remove from the heat; let stand for 5 minutes. Add eggs, one at a time, beating well after each addition. Beat until mixture is smooth and shiny.

2 Drop by rounded teaspoonfuls 2 in. apart onto greased baking sheets. Bake at 400° for 20-25 minutes or until golden brown. Remove puffs to wire racks. Immediately cut a slit in each for steam to escape. Cool. Split puffs and remove soft dough.

3 For filling, in a mixing bowl, whisk milk and pudding mix for 2 minutes. Refrigerate for 5 minutes. Fold in the whipped topping and chips. Fill cream puffs just before serving; replace tops. Dust with confectioners' sugar.

YIELD: ABOUT 2½ DOZEN.

Lean Haines, Lawrenceville, Georgia

French vanilla filling dotted with mini chocolate chips is sandwiched in puffy pastry for this elegantly sweet dessert. You could substitute white chocolate or chocolate pudding for the vanilla if you like.

brownie tarts

½ cup butter, softened

1 package (3 ounces) cream cheese, softened

1 cup all-purpose flour

FILLING:

½ cup semisweet chocolate chips

2 tablespoons butter

½ cup sugar

1 egg, beaten

1 teaspoon vanilla extract

½ cup chopped pecans, optional

Maraschino cherry halves, optional

1 In a mixing bowl, cream the butter and cream cheese. Add flour; mix well. Cover and refrigerate for 1 hour.

2 Shape into 1-in. balls. Place in ungreased miniature muffin cups; press into the bottom and up the sides to form a shell.

3 For filling, melt chocolate chips and butter in a small saucepan. Remove from the heat; stir in sugar, egg and vanilla. Add the pecans if desired. Spoon into shells.

4 Bake at 325° for 30-35 minutes or until brownies toothpick inserted near the center comes out clean. Cool for 10 minutes before removing from pans to wire racks. Garnish with cherries if desired.

YIELD: 2 DOZEN.

Sharon Wilkins, Grande Pointe, Ontario
I often take these chocolate goodies to potluck
dinners for our country dance club.

apricot crescents

1 cup cold butter

2 cups all-purpose flour

1 egg yolk

½ cup sour cream

½ cup apricot preserves

½ cup flaked coconut

¼ cup finely chopped pecans

Sugar

1 In a bowl, cut butter into flour until the mixture resembles coarse crumbs. Beat egg yolk and sour cream; add to crumb mixture and mix well. Cover and refrigerate for several hours or overnight.

2 Divide dough into fourths. On a sugared surface, roll each portion into a 10-in. circle. Turn dough over to sugar top side. Combine preserves, coconut and pecans; spread over circles. Cut each circle into 12 wedges and roll each wedge into a crescent shape, starting at the wide end. Sprinkle with sugar.

3 Place points down 1 in. apart on ungreased baking sheets. Bake at 350° for 15-17 minutes or until set and very lightly browned. Immediately remove to wire racks to cool.

YIELD: 4 DOZEN.

Tamyra Vest, Scottsburg, Virginia

When I was in college, my roommate's mother sent these flaky horns in a holiday care package. I've been making them ever since. When I mail them to my parents, I put an equal number in two tins labeled "his" and "hers" so there's no squabbling over who gets more.

apple walnut crescents

2 packages (8 ounces *each*) refrigerated crescent rolls

¼ cup sugar

1 tablespoon ground cinnamon

4 medium tart apples, peeled, cored and quartered

¼ cup chopped walnuts

¼ cup raisins, optional

¼ cup butter, melted

1 Unroll crescent roll dough and separate into 16 triangles. Combine sugar and cinnamon; sprinkle about ½ teaspoon on each triangle. Place an apple quarter near the short side and roll up. Place in a lightly greased 15-in. x 10-in. x 1-in. baking pan.

2 Press walnuts and raisins if desired into top of dough. Drizzle with butter. Sprinkle with the remaining cinnamon-sugar. Bake at 375° for 20-24 minutes or until golden brown. Serve warm.

YIELD: 16 SERVINGS.

Karen Petzold, Vassar, Michigan

A local apple orchard had a cook-off I wanted to enter, so I created these golden cinnamon treats. They're a snap to assemble with convenient crescent roll dough.

triple chocolate bundles

3 tablespoons semisweet chocolate chips

3 tablespoons vanilla *or* white chips

3 tablespoons milk chocolate chips

1 tube (8 ounces) refrigerated crescent rolls

Confectioners' sugar, optional

1 In a small bowl, combine the first three ingredients. Separate crescent dough into eight triangles. Place triangles on a work surface with the short edge toward you. For each bundle, place 1 tablespoon of chips in the center of each triangle. Bring top point over chips and tuck underneath dough. Fold side points over top, pressing to seal.

2 Place on an ungreased baking sheet. Bake at 375° for 10-12 minutes or until golden brown. Cool on a wire rack until serving. Sprinkle with sugar if desired.

YIELD: 8 BUNDLES.

Taste of Home Test Kitchen

No one will be able to resist three kinds of chocolate wrapped up in a fuss-free flaky dough. These are also delicious topped with a drizzle of melted chocolate.

puff pastry pillows

1 package (17.3 ounces) frozen puff pastry, thawed

1 egg

¼ cup milk

1 to 2 tablespoons coarse *or* granulated sugar

FILLING:

¼ cup all-purpose flour

1 cup milk

1 cup butter, softened

1 cup sugar

1 teaspoon vanilla extract

½ teaspoon almond extract

¼ teaspoon salt

1 Carefully open each puff pastry sheet. Cut each sheet of pastry at creases, forming 3 strips. Cut each strip widthwise into 7 pieces.

2 Combine egg and milk; lightly brush egg mixture over pastry. Sprinkle with sugar. Place on lightly greased baking sheets. Bake at 400° for 10-12 minutes or until golden brown. Remove to wire racks to cool. Split into top and bottom halves.

3 In a saucepan, combine the flour and milk until smooth. Bring to a boil over medium heat; cook and stir for 1 minute or until thickened. Cool.

4 Transfer to a mixing bowl; beat in the butter, sugar, vanilla, almond extract and salt until light and fluffy, about 10 minutes. Spread 1 tablespoonful on bottom half of each pastry; replace tops. Store in refrigerator.

YIELD: ABOUT 3½ DOZEN.

Robert Ryan, Newton, Iowa

My family and co-workers love these pretty, sweet treats. By using prepared puff pastry you have a fun dessert without much fuss.

pretty petits fours

¼ cup butter, softened

¼ cup shortening

1 cup sugar

1 teaspoon vanilla extract

1⅓ cups all-purpose flour

2 teaspoons baking powder

½ teaspoon salt

⅔ cup milk

3 egg whites

GLAZE:

2 pounds confectioners' sugar

⅔ cup plus 2 tablespoons water

2 teaspoons orange extract

FROSTING:

6 tablespoons butter, softened

2 tablespoons shortening

½ teaspoon vanilla extract

3 cups confectioners' sugar

3 to 4 tablespoons milk

Pink and green gel, liquid *or* paste food
    coloring

1 In a large mixing bowl, cream the butter, shortening and sugar. Beat in vanilla. Combine the flour, baking powder and salt add to creamed mixture alternately with milk. In a small mixing bowl, beat egg whites until soft peaks form; gently fold into batter.

2 Pour into a greased 9-in. square baking pan. Bake at 350° for 20-25 minutes or until a toothpick inserted near the center comes out clean. Cool for 10 minutes before removing from pan to a wire rack to cool completely.

3 Cut a thin slice off each side of cake. Cut cake into 1¼-in. squares. Place ½ in. apart on a rack in a 15-in. x 10-in. x 1-in. pan.

4 In a mixing bowl, combine glaze ingredients. Beat on low speed just until blended; beat on high until smooth. Apply glaze evenly over tops and sides of cake squares, allowing excess to drip off. Let dry. Repeat if necessary to thoroughly coat squares. Let dry completely.

5 For frosting, in a mixing bowl, cream the butter, shortening and vanilla. Beat in confectioners' sugar and enough milk to achieve desired consistency. Place ½ cup each in two bowls; tint one portion pink and one green.

6 Cut a small hole in the corner of a pastry or plastic bag; insert #104 tip. Fill with pink frosting; pipe a rosebud on each petit four. Insert #3 round tip into another pastry or plastic bag; fill with green frosting. Pipe a leaf under each rose.

YIELD: 2½ DOZEN (3 CUPS FROSTING).

Taste of Home Test Kitchen

Add a delicate touch to your dessert table with these bite-size cakes.

party pecan pies

1 cup butter, softened

1 package (8 ounces) cream cheese, softened

2 cups all-purpose flour

FILLING:

2 cups chopped pecans

1½ cups packed brown sugar

2 eggs, beaten

2 tablespoons butter, melted

2 teaspoons vanilla extract

1 In a mixing bowl, beat butter and cream cheese. Gradually add flour; mix well. Cover and refrigerate for 1 hour.

2 Press tablespoonfuls of dough into the bottom and up the sides of ungreased miniature muffin cups to form shells; set aside. Combine filling ingredients in a mixing bowl; mix well. Spoon about 1 heaping teaspoon into each shell.

3 Bake at 325° for 25-30 minutes or until crust is brown and filling is set. Cool for 10 minutes before removing from pans to wire racks.

YIELD: ABOUT 4 DOZEN.

Judy Theriot, Pierre Part, Louisiana

Though they're small, these pleasing "pies" are packed with flavor and sized right for a buffet. What's more, they can be stored in the freezer to make party or gift preparations that much easier.

miniature almond tarts

1 cup butter, softened

2 packages (3 ounces *each*) cream cheese, softened

2 cups all-purpose flour

FILLING:

  6 ounces almond paste, crumbled

  2 eggs, beaten

  1/2 cup sugar

FROSTING:

1 1/2 cups confectioners' sugar

  3 tablespoons butter, softened

  4 to 5 teaspoons milk

Maraschino cherry halves (about 48)

1 In a mixing bowl, cream the butter and cream cheese. Add flour; mix well. Cover and refrigerate for 1 hour.

2 Shape into 1-in. balls. Place in ungreased miniature muffin cups; press into the bottom and up the sides to form a shell.

3 For filling, combine the almond paste, eggs and sugar in a mixing bowl. Beat on low speed until blended. Fill each shell with about 1 1/2 teaspoons filling.

4 Bake at 325° for 25-30 minutes or until edges are golden brown. Cool for 10 minutes before removing to wire racks to cool completely.

5 For frosting, combine the confectioners' sugar, butter and enough milk to achieve desired consistency. Pipe or spread over tarts. Top each with a cherry half.

YIELD: ABOUT 4 DOZEN.

Karen Van Den Berge, Holland, Michigan

My family requests these adorable little tarts at the holidays. I always enjoy making them since the almond paste in the filling reflects our Dutch heritage, plus they're popular at special gatherings.

alphabetical recipe index

Refer to this index for a complete alphabetical listing of all the recipes in this book.

general recipe index

This handy index lists every recipe by food category and/or major ingredient, so you can easily locate recipes to suit your needs.

Pesto Cream Cheese Spread, 42
Raspberry Cheese Spread, 35
Roasted Goat Cheese with Garlic, 43
Sausage Cheese Squares, 148
Savory Cheese Cutouts, 208
Spinach-Cheese Mushroom Caps, 140
Sweet Cheese Ball, 21
Tangy Mozzarella Bites, 215
Tiered Cheese Slices, 36

cheese balls, slices & cheesecake
Crabmeat Appetizer Cheesecake, 30
Ham Cream Cheese Balls, 26
Sweet Cheese Ball, 21
Tiered Cheese Slices, 36

chicken
Bandito Chicken Wings, 115
Chicken Bacon Bites, 132
Chicken French Bread Pizza, 99
Chicken Ham Pinwheels, 198
Chicken Meatball Appetizers, 127
Chicken Nut Puffs, 169
Chicken Quesadillas, 102
Chicken Salad Cups, 49
Chicken Satay, 116
Coconut Chicken Bites, 127
Curried Chicken Tea Sandwiches, 94
Dijon Chicken Liver Pate, 37
Empanditas, 79
Garlic-Cheese Chicken Wings, 122
Nuggets with Chili Sauce, 125
Orange-Glazed Chicken Wings, 129
Sesame Chicken Bites, 130
Southwestern Chicken Pizza, 83
Tempura Chicken Wings, 136

chocolate
Brownie Tarts, 243
Chocolaty Popcorn, 235
Orange Chocolate Fondue, 41
Peanut Butter Chocolate Pretzels, 222
Triple Chocolate Bundles, 245
White Chocolate Party Mix, 224

corn
Calico Corn Salsa, 14
Fried Corn Balls, 153

cranberries
Berry Nut Tarts, 239
Cranberry Camembert Pizza, 110
Cranberry Meatballs and Sausage, 114
Hot and Spicy Cranberry Dip, 27
Tiered Cheese Slices, 36
Turkey Tortilla Spirals, 82

cucumbers
Asian Spring Rolls, 196
Beef Canapes with Cucumber Sauce, 184
Cucumber Canapes, 201
Cucumber Ham Roll-Ups, 203
Cucumber Whimsies, 213

desserts
Apple Walnut Crescents, 245
Apricot Crescents, 244
Berry Nut Tarts, 239
Brownie Tarts, 243
Cheese-Filled Shortbread Tartlets, 240
French Vanilla Cream Puffs, 242
Marmalade Turnovers, 241
Miniature Almond Tarts, 249
Party Pecan Pies, 248
Pretty Petits Fours, 247
Puff Pastry Pillows, 246
Strawberry Cookie Tarts, 241
Sugared Raisin Pear Diamonds, 238
Triple Chocolate Bundles, 245

dips (also see salsa)
Cold Dips
Festive Vegetable Dip, 16
Feta Olive Dip, 33
Guacamole Dip, 45
Roasted Eggplant Dip, 25
Salsa Guacamole, 37
Six-Layer Dip, 34

Warm Dips
Baked Spinach Dip in Bread, 22
Caramel Peanut Butter Dip, 18
Chorizo Cheese Dip, 27
Cider Cheese Fondue, 20
Hot and Spicy Cranberry Dip, 27
Orange Chocolate Fondue, 41

egg & spring rolls
Asian Spring Rolls, 196
Chorizo-Queso Egg Rolls, 53
Crispy Crab Rangoon, 76
Korean Wontons, 55
Pizza Rolls, 65
Southwestern Appetizer Triangles, 58
Veggie Shrimp Egg Rolls, 66

eggs
Bite-Size Crab Quiches, 71
Cheddar Artichoke
  Quiche Cups, 146
Guacamole-Stuffed Eggs, 203
Herbed Deviled Eggs, 191
Mini Bacon Quiches, 77
Party Puffs, 187
Petite Sausage Quiches, 52
Pickled Eggs and Beets, 197
Sweet-Sour Deviled Eggs, 204
Veggie Wonton Quiches, 57

fruit (also see specific kinds)
Fruit 'n' Cheese Kabobs, 210
Mixed Fruit Salsa, 17

ground beef
Bacon Nachos, 161
Enchilada Meatballs, 118
Ginger Meatballs, 123
Glazed Meatballs, 121
Honey-Garlic Glazed Meatballs, 126
Korean Wontons, 55
Southwestern Appetizer Triangles, 58
Veggie Nachos, 176